Global Chaos

 **Marshall Cavendish**
Benchmark
New York

Other Marshall Cavendish Offices:
Marshall Cavendish International (Asia) Private Limited, 1 New Industrial Road, Singapore 536196 • Marshall Cavendish International (Thailand) Co Ltd. 253 Asoke, 12th Flr, Sukhumvit 21 Road, Klongtoey Nua, Wattana, Bangkok 10110, Thailand • Marshall Cavendish (Malaysia) Sdn Bhd, Times Subang, Lot 46, Subang Hi-Tech Industrial Park, Batu Tiga, 40000 Shah Alam, Selangor Darul Ehsan, Malaysia

Marshall Cavendish is a trademark of Times Publishing Limited

All websites were available and accurate when this book was sent to press.

Library of Congress Cataloging-in-Publication Data

Global chaos.
     p. cm. -- (World War II)
  Summary: "Covers the events of World War II, including action in Italy and the Mediterranean; the Nazi State; Axis, Allied, and U.S. home fronts; and the Holocaust"---Provided by publisher.
  Includes bibliographical references and index.

  ISBN 978-0-7614-4948-5
  1. World War, 1939-1945--Campaigns--Juvenile literature. 2. World War, 1939-1945--Europe--Juvenile literature. 3. World War, 1939-1945--Social aspects--Juvenile literature.
  D743.7.G55 2011
  940.53--dc22
                        2010012734

Senior Editor: Deborah Grahame-Smith
Publisher: Michelle Bisson
Art Director: Anahid Hamparian
Series Designer: Bill Smith Group

PICTURE CREDITS
Associated Press: 12 (Staff/Worth), 19, 24, 52, 54, 116
Dreamstime.com: 83 (Martinspurny)
Library of Congress: 7, 14, 20, 44, 45, 46, 50, 54, 71, 79, 93, 97, 106, 112, 113, 115, 122
National Archives and Records: 10
Robert Hunt Library: 4, 30, 72, 88, 105
United States Air Force: 34
United States Coast Guard: 31
United States Navy: 22, 36
Shutterstock: Cover (Ivan Cholakov Gostock-dot-net), 32 (william m park), 38 (James Steidl), 70 (posztos [colorlab hu])

Additional imagery provided by U.S. Army, Joseph Gary Sheahan, 1944, Dreamstime.com, Shutterstock.com.

Printed in Malaysia (T)
135642

Contents

▶British troops advance past a blazing gasoline dump on the island of Pantelleria in June 1943. Allies had continuously bombed the island for more than one hundred hours.

1 Italy and the Mediterranean, 1942 to 1943

KEY PEOPLE		KEY PLACES
General George Patton	Field Marshal Albrecht Kesserling	Sicily
Field Marshal Bernard Montgomery	General Vittorio Ambrosio	Salerno
General Alfredo Guzzoni	Benito Mussolini	Taranto
	Marshal Pietro Badoglio	
	General Mark Clark	

In 1943, debate raged between the British and U.S. over opening a European front. President Roosevelt felt that a large-scale Italian invasion would drain Allied resources. These resources, he thought, would be better used in a northern European campaign.

At the Trident Conference in Washington, D.C, Roosevelt, British prime minister Winston Churchill, and others engaged in long debates. These debates resulted in a compromise. The Italian campaign would proceed. But a European attack through France would follow in spring 1944.

Before mounting an invasion of Italy, the Allies would need to control the mountainous island of Sicily. The first step was to capture the Italian island fortress of Pantelleria. During the first two weeks of June 1943, Allied air power pounded Pantelleria. About 6,550 tons of bombs were dropped in six days. On June 12 the Italians surrendered.

Operation Husky

Operation Husky, the invasion of Sicily, was the responsibility of the Fifteenth Army Group, led by British general Harold Alexander. It had two main forces—the U.S. Seventh Army, under General George Patton, and the British Eighth Army, led by Field Marshal Bernard Montgomery.

Allied commanders decided to concentrate on the southeastern corner of the island. The Eighth Army would land on the tip of Sicily. Patton's Seventh Army would invade the coastal strip 25 miles (40 km) west of the Eighth Army. Admiral Sir Andrew Cunningham of the British Royal Navy was in charge of 2,590 ships. Operation Husky would be the largest amphibious invasion ever. Not even the Normandy landings of June 1944 exceeded it. About 478,000 British and American troops landed in three days.

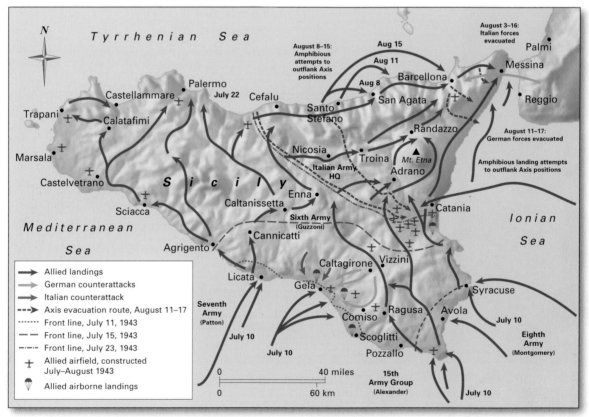

The Allied invasion of Sicily had the code name Operation Husky. The Allies believed that control of the island was important in the invasion of the mainland of Italy.

THE SARDINIA DECEPTION: OPERATION MINCEMEAT

Operation Mincemeat was one of the most unusual deceptions of World War II. During the buildup to Operation Husky, British intelligence wanted to mislead Hitler and his staff about the invasion plan. Germany thought Sicily was the most obvious way for the Allies to enter southern Europe. But the island of Sardinia was another possibility.

To convince Hitler that Sardinia was the Allied objective, two British intelligence officers came up with a gruesome plan, code-named Operation Mincemeat. The corpse of a London man received the identity of a British military courier, a Major Martin. His corpse was dressed in full uniform and equipped with false papers hinting that Sicily would be a diversion from the main invasion at Sardinia. The corpse was placed off the coast of Spain to make it look as if it had come from a downed aircraft. It then washed ashore.

Details of "Major Martin" soon filtered to Berlin. In response, the 90th Panzergrenadier Division and a Waffen SS brigade were sent to Sardinia. The 1st Panzer Division was sent to Greece. The Italian forces on Sicily were concentrated on the northern coast of the island facing Sardinia. As a result of the deception, the initial invasion of Sicily from the southeast was easy for the Allies. Operation Mincemeat was successful.

Operation Husky began on July 10, 1943. The naval landing was preceded by drops of airborne troops on the southern coast. The drops encountered strong winds and antiaircraft fire, scattering the paratroopers over a large area. The wind dramatically affected glider landings, with forty-seven British gliders crashing straight into the sea.

The amphibious landings were more successful. After a large naval and air bombardment, the landing craft brought thousands of men ashore. Most of the Italian defenders surrendered en masse.

In the amphibious invasion of Sicily, troops debark from the transports that are 4 miles (6.5 km) off shore. Fire from naval and air bombardment burns along the coast.

The defense of Sicily rested with General Alfredo Guzzoni's Italian Sixth Army. At this stage of the war the Sixth Army was weak. Many of its soldiers were native Sicilians. Presumably, they would fight hard for their homeland. In fact, most of the native Sicilians did not want to fight in a war they no longer believed in. Guzzoni also had overall command of two German units: the 15th Panzergrenadier Division and the Hermann Göring Panzer Division. Both German divisions had little equipment after the North Africa campaign. But they did have strong soldiers.

Axis resistance toughened on July 11 and 12. The Hermann Göring Panzer Division drove down from Caltagirone and attacked the U.S. 1st Infantry Division and U.S. Rangers. The attack used Tiger tanks and came within a half-mile (1 km) of the U.S. beachhead. Two cruisers and six destroyers shelled the German units, destroying about thirty tanks in the attack. On July 12 the 15th Panzergrenadier Division took over the defense of the American-invaded sector. The Hermann Göring Division was sent to deal with the British advance up the east coast.

By July 14 the Allied situation looked more promising. The American and British forces met up to control airfields at Ragusa and Comiso.

By July 14 the Allied situation looked more promising. The American and British forces met up to control airfields at Ragusa and Comiso. The airfields allowed the Allies to extend their air superiority still more—4,000 Allied aircraft faced fewer than 600 Axis aircraft.

Not everything, however, was working in the Allies' favor. Field Marshal Albrecht Kesselring, commander in chief of German forces in Italy, had reinforced Sicily with two paratroop regiments and the 29th Panzergrenadier Division. Command of German forces on Sicily had passed from General Guzzoni to Colonel-General H. V. Hube. The reinforcements and change in leadership toughened resistance. On July 14 British paratroopers and commandos were dropped to take the Primasole bridge, straddling the Simeto River. It so happened that German paratroopers were landing to the north. Though the British took the bridge, the German paratroopers fought them off and then held off the main Allied forces for three more days.

RAYMOND MITCHELL

Raymond Mitchell, a Royal Marine Commando, took part in the invasion of Sicily. Here he describes the realities of house-to-house fighting shortly after the landings.

Harry and Bill ranged themselves on either side of the doorway, rifles cocked, bayonets fixed, all ready to charge in. The officer and sergeant were also against the wall with pistols in their hands. I had positioned myself, in accordance with the appropriate paragraph of the training manual, directly in front of the door and about two yards away, down on one knee, tommy-gun all set to fire, finger on the trigger. Shep waved his gun, signaling, "Here goes!", fired two rounds into the lock and crashed the door open with his foot. As he stepped to one side I was in the doorway, my spluttering gun spraying bullets into the black interior.

Hardly had I stepped back to allow the rifleman to take over than the terrified screams of two or three children rang out from the darkness. "Good God! You've killed some kids!" The thought had barely formed itself in my brain before everything became completely silent once more. Was it some kind of a trap? Moving cautiously inside, weapons at the ready, we found the whole family of father, mother, and three or more children all cowering in one large bed. Fortunately, for my sake as well as theirs, it was against the front wall, behind the door we had just forced open. All were scared out of their wits but, mercifully, completely unharmed. My heart started beating again—thank God, we hadn't used a grenade!

Extract taken from *Sicily and Salerno, 1943* with *41 Royal Marines Commando* by Raymond Mitchell, Robert Hale Ltd, 1994.

After taking Catania, just above the Primasole bridge, the Eighth Army ground to a halt around Mount Etna.

In response, Montgomery redirected his force to the west, while Patton's Seventh Army drove to the northwest corner of Sicily to capture Trapani, Castellammare, and Palermo, the Sicilian capital, on July 22. From there Patton headed across the coastline toward Messina. German forces stopped the advance about 40 miles (64 km) from Messina. Cleverly, Patton was able to bypass the German defenses. He resumed his advance on Messina. During August two new Allied infantry divisions joined the campaign. The Axis hold on Sicily was no longer sustainable. Guzzoni and Kesselring ordered Italian and German troops to escape to mainland Italy. Two-thirds of the Axis forces in Sicily escaped, along with 17,000 tons of equipment.

On August 17, 1943, the U.S. 3rd Infantry Division entered Messina shortly ahead of the British.

The Allies had thrown German and Italian forces out of Sicily. Still, the British and Americans suffered 2,721 and 2,811 dead respectively. Such losses hinted at what Allied soldiers would face later on the Italian mainland.

The Downfall of Mussolini

While the Allies were battling through Sicily, the Italian leader, Benito Mussolini, was fighting his own battle. The war was not going Italy's way. By July 1943 Italy had lost its African empire. Its troops had suffered huge losses in Russia and the Balkans. Because of its many overseas commitments, Italy was guarded by only twenty divisions, most with old arms. The air force was outdated. The Italian navy had lost more than 35,000 sailors. Most in the government knew that the war was lost.

General George Patton and Lieutenant Colonel Lyle Bernard discuss military strategy. In the background the direction arrow points the way to Messina, Italy. General Patton's strategy allowed the Allies to bypass German defenses.

Between December 1942 and April 1943, Mussolini had asked Hitler many times to make peace with the Soviet Union. Mussolini wanted Hitler to use German forces in southern Europe. Hitler refused. To the rest of his government, Mussolini appeared weak. Many felt that he would have to be removed. In early 1943 General Vittorio Ambrosio, chief of the Italian Supreme General Staff, explained to Mussolini that Italy could not resist an invasion. He recommended that Mussolini pull Italy out of the war. Ambrosio and Mussolini went to a final conference with Hitler on July 19. Ambrosio hoped to hear Mussolini tell Hitler that, unless Germany provided reinforcements, Italy could no longer fight. Through a mixture of pride and weakness, Mussolini said nothing.

> *To the rest of his government, Mussolini appeared weak.*

Ambrosio, Marshal Pietro Badoglio, a former chief of the Italian Supreme General Staff, and the Italian royal family then plotted to topple Mussolini. After a meeting in Rome of the Fascist Ground Council on July 24, 1943, Mussolini was arrested and taken to the island of Ponza. Marshal Badoglio took over as head of the Italian state.

Badoglio and his new government then secretly asked the Allies for an armistice. Hitler had long worried that the Italians might do just this. In July 1943 Field Marshal Erwin Rommel led eight German infantry divisions across the Italian border. They occupied the mountainous north. Also, the 2nd Parachute Division and 3rd Panzergrenadier Division were at Ostia, near Rome. They would disarm Rome's garrisons and capture key government figures in the event of an armistice.

On September 3, 1943, the day the Allies began their invasion of mainland Italy, General Giuseppe Castellano signed an armistice with the Allies on behalf of the Italian government and royal family. Fearing German action, however, the Italian government did not announce the armistice until September 9. When the armistice was announced, German troops marched into Rome. They disarmed the confused Italian units. The Italian king and government managed to escape and fled to the south. The Italian army collapsed. More than 650,000 former soldiers were deported to Germany by their former ally.

KEY
FIGURES

British army officer Harold Alexander (1891–1961) became one of the most senior Allied leaders of World War II. He was born a British aristocrat and had served in World War I. He became a British general in 1937.

After he handled the Dunkirk evacuation in May–June 1940, Alexander was promoted to lieutenant general. He took commanding roles in the Allied campaigns in Burma and North Africa. His leadership of the Eighteenth Army Group played a key part in the eventual surrender of the Axis forces in North Africa.

After the African campaign, Alexander became commander in chief of the Fifteenth Army Group for the invasion of Sicily in July 1943. He subsequently became Allied supreme commander in the Mediterranean, and was promoted to field marshal. In 1945 Alexander personally took the surrender of the German troops in Italy. He was knighted in 1942 and was made the Viscount of Tunis in 1946.

Some have criticized Alexander for blindly accepting some of the recommendations from Field Marshal Bernard Montgomery and for some of his other decisions in the Italian campaign. However, his strong and friendly personality made him a personal friend of Prime Minister Winston Churchill and a very respected Allied commander.

Field Marshal Harold Alexander

Baytown and Avalanche

The Allied campaign in mainland Italy was one of the most flawed operations of the war. Although Winston Churchill had initially thought of Italy as the "soft underbelly" of Axis-occupied Europe, it proved to be no such thing. The Allied Italian campaign turned out to be a difficult slog through a even more difficult terrain. The Allies were also fighting against a seasoned enemy. The German troops were commanded by Field Marshal

Kesselring, who had at his disposal eight large German divisions and the Tenth Army.

Tactical mistakes were made at the planning level. General Harold Alexander and General Dwight D. Eisenhower were the Allied leaders of the land forces, and Air Chief Marshal Arthur Tedder and Admiral Cunningham led the Allied air and sea forces. Their plan was for Montgomery's Eighth Army to move from Sicily onto the "toe" of Italy at Reggio di Calabria and advance from the south. This landing was intended to draw German reinforcements away from the main invasion force, the U.S. Fifth Army under General Mark Clark. These troops would be landing at the Gulf of Salerno, about 300 miles (483 km) to the north on the eastern coast of Italy.

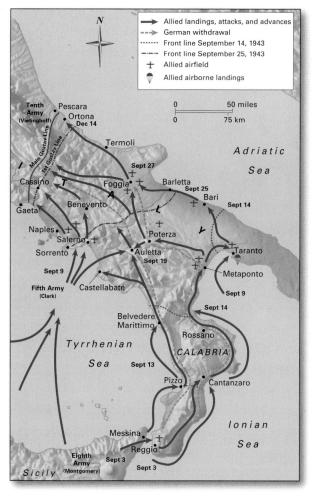

The Allies landed at Salerno and southern Italy in the Italian campaign, beginning in September 1943. The Allied plan failed to consider the difficult terrain along the coast.

GENERAL MARK CLARK

KEY FIGURES

General Mark Clark

General Mark Clark (1896–1984) was commander of the U.S. Fifth Army during the Italian campaign. A veteran of World War I, Clark rose to become deputy supreme commander for the North African landings of Operation Torch. He conducted dangerous secret missions with the French military authorities in the region. He was then promoted to lieutenant colonel.

In September 1943 Clark led the Fifth Army during the Salerno landings and showed great bravery. His performance in the Italian campaign, however, has been questioned. When told to surround the German Tenth Army in May 1944, Clark ignored the order and freed Rome. The Tenth Army then escaped and set up defensive positions in northern Italy. Clark's decision resulted in massive Allied casualties later on. Clark was also criticized for his assaults across the Rapido River in early 1944, costing more than 2,000 lives in twenty-four hours. Despite these incidents, in late 1944 Clark was promoted to commander of the Allied forces in Italy. While sometimes controversial, Clark was also respected as a forceful leader and an effective organizer.

The Allies' critical mistake was not making an amphibious invasion farther north than Salerno. The backbone of Italy is dominated by the Apennine Mountains. Only narrow strips of flat land lie on each coast. Travel through the mountains is difficult even today. Narrow hairpin roads are not ideal for major supply operations in wartime.

The main supply line of the Germans was the road that ran through Rome and followed the west coast. Had the Allies invaded higher up the west coast of Italy, they could have cut this supply route. This would have separated the German Tenth Army, under General van Vietinghoff, from mainland Europe. Prior to the landings, even Hitler seemed to think that the Tenth Army would be lost in the Italian campaign.

The Allies chose Salerno because air support would come from aircraft flying from Sicily and Malta. However, if the Allies had invaded farther north, German air and ground forces would probably have been unable to stop the Allies advance. The Allies could have also bypassed the German Gustav Line running coast to coast. Taking this series of defensive positions would cost the Allies large numbers of casualties in 1944. Ultimately, the Allies chose to send the Eighth Army through an unimportant and mountainous region of Italy. At the same time they landed the Fifth Army at well-defended but unimportant Salerno.

At 4:30 a.m. on September 3, 1943, Operation Baytown, the Eighth Army's invasion, began at Calabria. The undefended coastline had been smashed by heavy artillery fire and naval gunfire. The advance encountered no Germans whatsoever for the first 5 miles (8 km), and found only light resistance later on. The Germans had no orders to engage the invasion. They had, however, ruined roads and bridges and scattered booby traps in the path of the advancing Allies. It took the British 5th Division and Canadian 1st Division six days to reach Pizzo and Catanzaro—only 30 miles (48 km) into Italy.

Operation Avalanche was the code name for the Salerno landings, which began on September 9 at 3:30 a.m. under General Mark Clark. In the hope of achieving total surprise, the Allies had not done any preliminary bombardment. However, German spy aircraft had seen the approaching fleet on September 8. For the Salerno landings, the U.S. Fifth Army consisted of the U.S. VI Corps and the British X Corps. American forces would land in the south of the Gulf of Salerno around Paestum. The British and units of U.S. Rangers would land around Salerno. Facing the initial Allied attack was the 16th Panzer Division.

The Avalanche landings were a contrast to those made by Montgomery's Eighth Army troops, which had encountered little German resistance in their landings at Calabria. However, for the Fifth Army assault around Paestum, the U.S. 36th Division was under heavy enemy fire even before

The 46th and 56th divisions, which conducted the main landings, took heavy casualties.

the landing craft touched the beach. Only naval gunfire support let the troops gain control, while the German 16th Panzer Division turned north.

The British X Corps experience was similar. The 46th and 56th divisions, which conducted the main landings, took heavy casualties. Although they managed to establish a beachhead, they were unable to make any true advance. As night fell on September 9, 7 miles (11 km) of enemy-held territory still separated the British X Corps and U.S. VI Corps. British beachheads were just a quarter of a mile (0.6 km) deep. U.S. troops had only managed a 5-mile (8-km) advance to Capaccio.

Avalanche had not had a good first day. On the second day the U.S. 36th Division was reinforced by its reserve force, the 45th Division. Together they advanced 10 miles (16 km) inland, but were forced into retreat by the German counterattacks. The British were also fighting seesaw battles against German divisions pouring into the area, taking and then losing Battipaglia, 5 miles (8 km) out from the beachhead.

The battle for the Salerno beachheads reached its peak on September 13 and 14. The Allies remained pinned down under artillery and small-arms fire. On the evening of September 13 the Germans launched a counteroffensive between the British and American corps. On September 14–15 the situation improved because of American and British reinforcements. Allied ground-attack aircraft made about 2,000 sorties on September 14 alone. Eighteen battleships and many destroyers and cruisers shattered German armor from offshore.

The Push to the Gustav Line

By September 16 the bombardment and the constant buildup of Allied troops around Salerno led Kesselring to order a withdrawal. He began to pull his troops north toward the Gustav Line. The Gustav Line followed the line of the Rapido and Garigliano rivers before crossing the Apennines to the Adriatic coast of eastern Italy. It was studded with emplacements, bunkers, and defensive positions miles deep. This made it the most threatening obstacle to the Allied advance in Italy.

Meanwhile, events were unfolding in the south. The Eighth Army's advance from Calabria had been sluggish. By September 19, however, they reached Auletta near the Gulf of Salerno. There they met up with the forces of Avalanche.

In addition, on the first day of Avalanche the British 1st Airborne Division made another landing, code-named Operation Slapstick, at Taranto in far southeast Italy. Slapstick's objective was to secure ports at Taranto, Brindisi, and Bari. These could supply an Allied advance up the eastern side of Italy. The initial landing was unopposed. The British 78th Division landed at

In addition, on the first day of Avalanche the British 1st Airborne Division made another landing, code-named Operation Slapstick...

Bari on September 22. Its advance up the eastern coast was fairly easy. By September 27 the 78th Division had reached Foggia, opposite Naples.

On October 2–3 British commandos captured the port of Termoli. Seeing the danger in the east, Vietinghoff rushed the 16th Panzer Division to Termoli and tried to retake it on October 5. Although the British commandos were pushed to the edge of town, the Germans were driven into retreat. They withdrew to the Trigno River, 30 miles (48 km) north of Termoli. Meanwhile, Clark's Fifth Army was making slow progress from Salerno toward the Gustav Line. An offensive by the British 10th Corps on September 23 toward Naples battled against a German action. It took nine days to cover a little over 25 miles (40 km). The U.S. VI Corps had a similar experience. It wheeled to the east of Naples toward Benevento, 40 miles (64 km) from VI Corps' Salerno landing zones. Like the British, they had to battle German troops and overcome demolished or booby-trapped roads and bridges. On October 2 they finally entered Benevento. In three weeks of action following the Salerno landings the Allies had suffered more than 12,000 casualties.

During October, the Italian weather became harsh. Endless rain flooded ditches, rotted clothing, chilled troops, and made mountain tracks almost impassable. By the end of 1943 more than 40,000 Allied troops were hospitalized or withdrawn from action because of sickness made worse by the climate.

By October 8 both Allied forces squared up to the German defenses on the Volturno. The VI Corps began its assault on October 12, while the British were forced to make their assault about ten days later after they had been delayed by German resistance. By October 18 the Germans were retreating toward the Gustav Line, inflicting heavy casualties on the American infantry. The Volturno defense had served its purpose, delaying the Allied advance and buying time to prepare the defenses of the Gustav Line. Such was both the German resistance and the Italian weather that by November 15 General Alexander halted the offensive. He needed time to allow his battle-scarred troops to recover. Nearly 22,000 Allied troops had been reported lost in action, dead, wounded, or missing.

On the eastern side of Italy, Montgomery was having a tough time.

On the eastern side of Italy, Montgomery was having a tough time.

His troops managed to break through on the Trigno. Their next obstacle was the Sangro River. The main attempt to break across the Sangro began on November 28. The German defenders suffered a heavy softening-up attack from Allied air power and artillery. The Allies outnumbered the German defenders on the ground; by November 30 they had punched across the Sangro River.

Then came a difficult four-week advance resisted by the 90th Panzergrenadier Division and 26th Panzer Division. Though the Gustav Line was crossed, a series of river defenses slowed further progress and cost heavy Allied casualties. By the end of December the advance was brought to a halt 2 miles (3 km) north of Ortona and 7 miles (11 km) short of the Eighth Army's objective, Pescara. From Pescara a major east–west road route ran through to Rome. Its capture would have significantly helped the Allied campaign.

In the west, the Fifth Army's drive toward the Gustav Line started up again on November 20. Relying on superiority in troops and a great artillery advantage, the Allies inched slowly forward. In the beginning, the fighting was largely along Route 6, the main road to Rome. It involved the capture of several major mountain peaks, including Monte Camino, Monte La Diffensa, Monte Rotundo, and Monte Maggiore.

By December 7 the offensive was broadened across a 50-mile (80-km) front, but once again the Allies suffered many casualties for little progress. Because of severe weather, Allied air power could not be well used. By December 14 the offensive had ground to a halt roughly 5 miles (8 km) south of the Rapido River bordering the Gustav Line. Its troops and supplies were totally exhausted.

The Allied Italian campaign reached a stalemate. U.S. and British troops hunkered down in the freezing Italian winter. Many occupied positions in the mountains that gave no relief from wind, snow, rain, and mud. The cost of driving to the Gustav Line was high. The Allies suffered—over 50,000 casualties in the Fifth Army alone. Allied tactical failures and German resilience had hardened the "soft underbelly" of Italy. Much more blood remained to be spilled in the coming year.

In the Invasion of Sicily, Allied troops had to pull heavy artillery up narrow, hairpin mountain roads. In August 1943, these U.S. soldiers lug a large 155 mm gun behind their truck.

▶Merchant ships and the naval vessels that accompanied them made up an Allied convoy. Stopping German U-boat attacks upon Allied convoys was important in the Battle of the Atlantic.

2 The Battle of the Atlantic, 1942 to 1943

KEY PEOPLE	KEY PLACES	
❖ Admiral Karl Dönitz	🔲 Russia	Atlantic Ocean
🇺🇸 Admiral Ernest J. King	Arctic	

As far as Admiral Karl Dönitz was concerned, Hitler's declaration of war against the United States gave him a great opportunity. There would be fewer U.S. naval forces off the eastern seaboard of America as ships were sent to the Pacific theater. So the German submariners anticipated a few weeks of easy successes. By late 1941 Dönitz would have 250 submarines in service. However, orders from Hitler kept a large number of these craft out of the main Atlantic battles in the early days of fighting.

The Japanese attack on Pearl Harbor had been a complete surprise to the Germans. Dönitz had no U-boats ready to move into the waters off the East Coast of the United States. The Germans had two main types of combat U-boat: Type VII and Type IX. They had more of the Type VIIs, but only the larger Type IXs had a long enough range to operate off the U.S. coast. And finally, traveling there from the German submarine bases took three weeks. All this meant that Dönitz had only a small force in U.S. waters.

But the boats used a great deal of fuel fighting their first battles. So, in February 1942 the Germans put their first specially made supply submarines into service. These supply submarines played a vital role in increasing the range of the combat boats. In turn, the supply submarines became targets of the Allied forces.

German U-boats, such as this *U-3008* shown in port, were a menace to Allied shipping during the Battle of the Atlantic. The Allies improved their tactics and technology to gain the advantage.

Operation Drumroll

By mid-January 1942 Dönitz had twelve boats in position to begin what he called Operation Drumroll. He sent seven Type VII U-boats to waters near Newfoundland. They achieved very little, mainly because of the severe winter weather. The five Type IX U-boats sent to the East Coast did much better. They opened their attack on January 12, and by the end of the month had sunk more than thirty ships. The great successes went on. During the first three months of 1942 the Allies lost 2 million tons of shipping in all theaters. More than half fell to the ten to fifteen U-boats in action at any one time off the eastern United States. More than half the ships sunk in American waters were tankers carrying fuel from the Gulf of Mexico.

American Unpreparedness

The shipping losses amounted to a massacre that was made easier by American blunders. Lighthouses and buoys were kept fully lit, making German navigation simple. Coastal towns in Florida refused at first to black out streetlighting and advertising, fearing that a blackout would hurt their businesses. As a result, during that time period, the U-boats were able to sink ship after ship silhouetted against the glare. In April 1942 merchant ships began to sail in convoy off the eastern seaboard of the United States. It was well into the summer before the system extended to the Caribbean and the Gulf of Mexico.

By December 1941 the U.S. Navy should have had plans in place to protect shipping in America's home waters in case of war. Yet the U.S. Navy did not have enough ships to escort convoys properly. The navy did not realize that even weakly escorted convoys were far better than none. They also did not recognize that weak escort forces had to be concentrated with the merchant ships. That was where the U-boats would be.

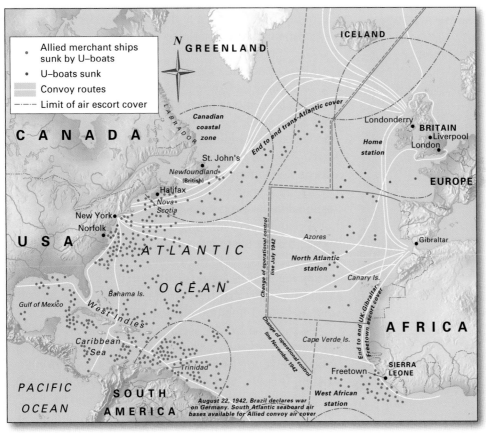

The clusters of red dots show how many Allied merchant ships were sunk by U-boats from January 1942 to February 1943 in the Battle of the Atlantic. The Allies lost dozens of ships.

The failure began at the top. Admiral Ernest J. King, appointed to head the U.S. Navy in December 1941, preferred to send resources to the Pacific. King was also difficult to work with—one of his own family said he was the most even-tempered man in the navy because he was always angry. King had little liking for anything outside the U.S. Navy, and he hated everything British. He preferred to set up American systems and organizations from scratch. Those weaknesses were very costly in early 1942, when Allied resources of escort ships were under great strain. This weakness was

ADMIRAL KARL DÖNITZ

Karl Dönitz

Admiral Karl Dönitz (1891–1980) was the creator of Germany's U-boat force and its commander until early 1943, when he was appointed commander in chief of the German navy.

Dönitz had been a submarine commander during World War I. He was taken prisoner by the British after his U-boat was sunk. He remained in the German navy after obtaining his freedom at the end of the war, and was later given the task of building a submarine force. This had to be achieved in secret, since Germany was denied submarines under the Treaty of Versailles. Dönitz, appointed the fleet's commander in 1935, was responsible for preparing it for World War II.

A popular and resourceful commander, Dönitz always did his best for his men. He varied tactics and maneuvered forces to outwit the enemy. His greatest failure was that he never realized that his codes had been broken, or that the command system that he set up made the U-boat force vulnerable as a result.

By the time Dönitz became commander in chief of the navy, Germany's surface fleet was just about out of action. He kept trying to devise new strategies for his existing U-boats, and worked to bring new and better types of vessels into service. Dönitz remained loyal to Hitler to the war's end, and Hitler appointed him as his successor shortly before his death in April 1945. Dönitz surrendered to the Allies a few days later. He was tried for war crimes after the war and received a ten-year prison sentence.

even worse in the Atlantic, because on February 1 the Germans changed the coding system used by their U-boats. The new codes would not be broken until December.

In early April the U.S. Navy finally started a convoy system for ships off the New England coast. These convoys linked up with those on the Canada–U.K. routes. In May the system was extended south to Florida. In the meantime losses continued to be quite high. So many tankers had been sunk that Admiral King ordered them into port in May until the new convoy system could begin.

So many tankers had been sunk that Admiral King ordered them into port in May until the new convoy system could begin.

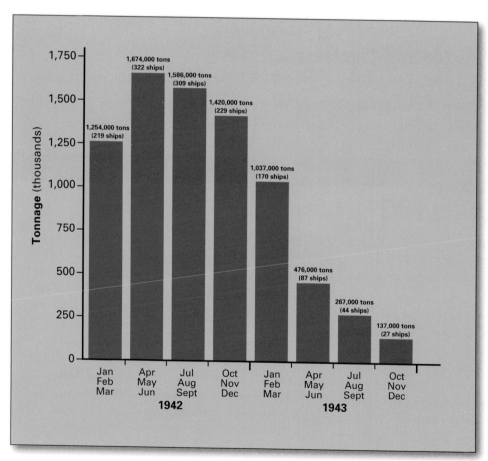

In the spring of 1942, the Allies lost over 1 million tons of shipping to German attacks. Those losses dramatically decreased as the Allies gained the upper hand in the Atlantic.

The British agreed to reduce the number of convoys on the main North Atlantic routes, cutting back their imports so that they could send some of their escort ships to help off the East Coast. These measures brought the sinkings in U.S. waters under control. Still, June 1942 turned out to be the worst month of the war for Allied shipping losses. Dönitz eventually abandoned operations off the East Coast in July. By then the defenders were well organized and up to good strength. In any case, as far back as May Dönitz had moved many of his U-boats to the Caribbean. He also mounted attacks off Africa and Brazil, keeping the Allied forces spread thin as the Allies attempted to cover potential targets. The sinkings off Brazil did, however, turn out to help the Allied cause. Brazil declared war on Germany in August, giving the Allies access to many good air bases there.

Hitler and the German Navy

As he did with army operations, Hitler often gave orders to his naval forces that were not properly thought out. He did not use his ships against the most important objectives. Throughout 1941 and 1942, for example, he sent

CODES AND CODE BREAKING

TECH

Code breaking played a vital role for both sides in the Battle of the Atlantic. The British were the best at exploiting what they picked up. Their code breakers led the attack on Germany's messages. The United States concentrated their efforts against Japan's systems. Any information was shared between U. S. and British commanders.

One of the strengths of the British code-breaking system was that it was under a single organization, the Government Code and Cypher School. The British also designed what were essentially early computers to help in the code-breaking process. The Germans never suspected the British or matched them.

The Germans had several code systems in use—one for Atlantic U-boats, one for major surface ships, and several others. The navy was the most careful and the Luftwaffe the least secure. They encoded messages on Enigma machines, which resembled complicated electric typewriters. The Enigma machines settings were changed daily. Each day, the British had to sift through millions of changes to identify the new settings.

Sometimes the Allies mounted operations that would provoke the Germans into disclosing codes. For example, Allied aircraft dropped mines near German bases to provoke the Germans into sending warning messages to their ships.

The British began to break German U-boat codes in the summer of 1941. The British sometimes could read the signals within hours of the Germans sending them. When the Germans introduced a new complication, the British could not read their codes for some time. Beginning in the summer of 1943 until the end of the war, the British could read the codes of the German war messages promptly and efficiently.

In the Battle of the Atlantic, although the Germans knew how much the British knew about U-boats in 1941 and 1943, they never realized how the codes had been broken. They thought that British radar was responsible. Britain continued to be successful in code breaking until the end of the war.

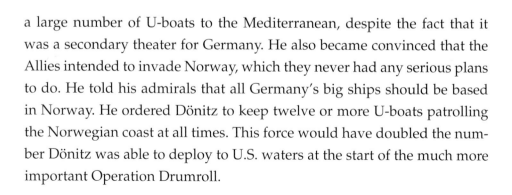

a large number of U-boats to the Mediterranean, despite the fact that it was a secondary theater for Germany. He also became convinced that the Allies intended to invade Norway, which they never had any serious plans to do. He told his admirals that all Germany's big ships should be based in Norway. He ordered Dönitz to keep twelve or more U-boats patrolling the Norwegian coast at all times. This force would have doubled the number Dönitz was able to deploy to U.S. waters at the start of the much more important Operation Drumroll.

LIFE ABOARD A U-BOAT

PEOPLE AND WAR

Germany's U-boats were fairly well designed, but at the expense of keeping their crews comfortable. When starting out on a mission, it was vital to carry as much fuel, food and torpedoes as possible. Every corner of the boat was crammed with stores, including crew bunks.

Patrols lasted at least three weeks, and often much longer. No one washed or shaved throughout this time. There was barely enough water for drinking and cooking. A single toilet was shared by the roughly fifty-man crew. The toilet could be used only when the boat was on the surface. Sometimes a boat had to stay submerged for at least twenty-four hours.

The smell of unwashed bodies and cans of waste combined with the smell of diesel oil and chlorine (if seawater got into the U-boat's batteries) made the U-boat nearly insufferable. Some crew members must have been driven mad by the stench.

Then there was fear: the panic of a crash dive when an aircraft approached, or the long agony of being hunted by escort ships. U-boats moved blindly underwater, hearing the constant *ping-ping* as sonar from surface ships searched for them. They waited tensely while depth charges sunk nearby, perhaps wondering if the one they heard would be the very one to crack open the hull and admit the crushing weight of seawater.

Above all, especially later in the war, the U-boat crews knew that their chances of survival were poor. Germany sent almost 1,200 U-boats into action. About one-fourth of these were destroyed before completing their first active patrol. Three-fourths of the men who served in U-boats were killed in the course of the war.

Hitler was not able to use Germany's battleships effectively. *Tirpitz*, a sister ship of *Bismarck*, was declared operational at the start of 1942. *Scharnhorst*, *Gneisenau*, and *Prinz Eugen* were at Brest in western France after earlier operations. Hitler decided that they should all be based in Norway. Deploying *Tirpitz* was easy, but he fretted over the best way to get the other ships there—through the open North Atlantic and around the north of the British Isles, or through the English Channel under the noses of the British. The Germans chose the bold option, code-named Operation Cerberus. On February 12, 1942, they got away with it, through a combination of good planning, several strokes of luck, and blunders by the British.

To have the pride of the German navy sail within 20 miles (32 km) of the British coast seemed like an insult to the British. But all three German ships were either damaged in the process or struck shortly afterward by air or submarine attacks. Only *Scharnhorst* would ever see action again. When the ships were in

To have the pride of the German navy sail within 20 miles (32 km) of the British coast seemed like an insult to the British.

Brest it had been nearly impossible for the British to keep them from slipping out into the Atlantic to attack the trade routes. Ships in Norway were still a menace, but easier to block.

Arctic Convoys

In August 1941 the British started sending convoys through the Arctic to northern Russia. From the moment Hitler attacked Russia in June 1941, Soviet leader Joseph Stalin begged for help from Britain and the United States. He needed supplies, but above all he wanted an invasion of German-occupied Europe. American and British leaders decided that the second front against Germany would have to wait. As a result, sending supplies to Russia to prevent a German victory there became even more important.

Other routes to Russia would become more important later in the war. In all, the Allies sent forty convoys to and from northern Russia. The convoys traveled a 2,000-mile (3,200-km) journey to or from Britain or Iceland. Much of the route passed within 300 miles (480 km) of German bases in northern Norway. The weather was harsh more often than not, with severe storms, ice, and fog. Any good summer weather at such high latitudes meant almost twenty-four-hour daylight for German attack forces. Despite the difficulties faced by the convoys, the Russians did next to nothing to help with support or with port facilities. The first few convoys got through without trouble. But from the spring of 1942, the Germans stepped up their attacks. Many merchant ships and escorting warships were sunk, and in July there was a disaster. Two-thirds of the ships in convoy PQ.17 were sunk after commanders ordered the convoy to split up because they feared a German battlegroup was in the area. The next in the series, PQ.18, lost one-third of its cargo ships. Shortly after these disasters, the Germans moved many aircraft from Norway to the Mediterranean to oppose the Allied invasion of North Africa, reducing the danger of German attacks.

At the end of 1942 there was a great Allied success in the Arctic. On December 31, the Germans tried to intercept the convoy JW.51B with the *Lützow*, the heavy cruiser *Admiral Hipper*, and a force of destroyers. These ships greatly outgunned the convoy's escort. The British covering force was too far away to come into action. The German admiral was cautious, however, and was fooled into retreating by the tactics of the smaller British cruisers and destroyers. Hitler was furious. This failure confirmed for Hitler how useless his surface ships were. Admiral Raeder, commander in chief of the German navy, resigned and was replaced by Admiral Dönitz. With the head of the U-boat force in charge of the whole navy it was clear where the focus of German naval operations would lie.

German U-boats torpedoed the Allied convoy fleet PQ.17. These survivors wait for further rescue. In the biggest disaster of the war, the Allies lost twenty-four ships and 153 men were killed.

The Greatest Convoy Battles

Even when his forces were in action off the American coast, Dönitz did not give up attacks on the main North Atlantic convoys. In the late summer and early fall of 1942 he increased the attacks again. The German U-boat force was still growing. More than one hundred boats were put into operation in the fall and two hundred by the end of the year. Dönitz now had the strength he had long believed would make a decisive victory possible. He also had the vital upper hand in the code-breaking struggle—for now.

Several developments on the Allied side meant Germany did not always have the upper hand. Better Allied training meant that escort ships were working together better than before. Radar and antisubmarine weapons were also improved. Canadian forces now made up almost half of the Allied strength in the North Atlantic. For a time the Canadians lagged behind the British. The Canadian navy had expanded more rapidly than its training system, but now they were catching up. Better radar and other equipment also meant that British aircraft were able to strike at U-boats crossing the Bay of Biscay to and from their bases in France. Nevertheless, American and British air force leaders and Admiral King refused to allow more than a handful of long-range aircraft to the main convoy routes.

In this illustration, a "Kingfisher" patrol plane surprises a German U-boat off the Atlantic coast. The submarine has surfaced to pick up stragglers from a downed convoy just on the horizon.

TECH

A sonar screen shows six U-boats in the vicinity. The small blips on the sonar screen give their bearing, but not their depth. Sinking U-boats might take hours.

World War II technology gave escort ships three ways of detecting U-boats: radar, radio direction finding, and sonar.

Radar was in its infancy when the war began. Few ships had radar, and the operating wavelengths that could not detect anything as small as a surfaced submarine. The first effective ship and aircraft radars were introduced in 1941, but did not become common until later. U-boats were never fitted with good radar, but they did have radar detectors that could warn of an approaching Allied ship or aircraft.

Radio direction finding was well known in all countries before the war. But British scientists succeeded in developing high-frequency direction-finding (HF/DF for short, or "Huff-Duff" as it was properly known) equipment small enough to fit aboard ship. This gave convoy escorts accurate positions for any nearby U-boats using their radios, whether or not the German codes were being read.

Sonar (known as Asdic by the British during World War II) was a system of sending out underwater pulses of sound from a ship and detecting when they were reflected back by a submarine. Wartime sonar had a range of less than 1 mile (1,600 m) and could only give a bearing for a suspected U-boat. It could not tell how deep the U-boat might be. Sonar also did not work when the U-boat was too close. Therefore it was useful only when when depth charges needed were set and fired. Even when a U-boat had been accurately detected, destroying the U-boat might take hours of attacks and many depth charges.

Today's electronic equipment is so reliable that it's difficult to consider how crude and fragile such things were in the 1940s. When new equipment was invented, the first examples were often hand-built from whatever was available, rather than custom designed. Maintenance systems were worked out later, and operators had to learn on the job. There were breakdowns and damage was caused by bad weather. Allied scientists definitely won the electronic war in the Battle of the Atlantic, but very often a sharp pair of eyes was the only detection available.

Allied shipping losses peaked again in November 1942, partly because many escort ships were protecting ships in Operation Torch. The greatest convoy battles came in February and March 1943. In March, for example, the convoys SC.122 and HX.229, totaling ninety merchant ships and sixteen escorts, were attacked by packs that eventually included thirty-eight U-boats. In a mid-Atlantic running battle lasting several days and nights, the convoys lost twenty-two ships in return for only one U-boat destroyed. It was a major German victory. Some Allied leaders feared that it was a sign that the Germans were going to win the Battle of the Atlantic. But within a few weeks the situation changed completely.

Defeat of the U-boats

Neither side had a definite advantage in April's battles, but in early May all forty-five ships of convoy SC.130 got through. The Germans lost forty-one U-boats during the month, more than double their worst loss in any earlier month of the war. Dönitz realized he had been defeated. On May 22 he ordered all North Atlantic U-boats to give up convoy attacks.

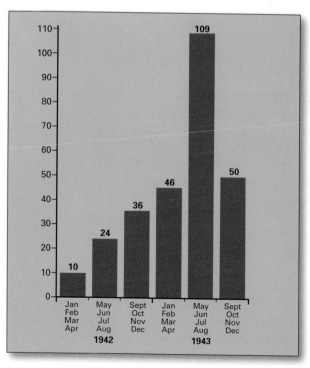

As Allied navies grew more successful in 1942 and 1943, German U-boat losses increased. In the late spring and summer of 1943 German U-boat losses doubled.

VERY LONG RANGE AIRCRAFT

The B-24 Liberator

During World War II, U-boats sank only twenty-five Allied ships in the Atlantic when both air and surface escorts were present. Yet the Allied leaders were slow to deploy more than a handful of aircraft in support.

The best Very Long Range (VLR) aircraft of the war was the American-made Consolidated Liberator. The VLR variants of the Liberator could fly missions of up to twenty hours, which allowed them several hours in action over a convoy 1,000 miles (1,600 km) from their bases. This range made them ideal to cover, or at least minimize, the "air gap" in the mid-Atlantic. It took until the late spring of 1943, however, before many VLR aircraft were used. At the climax of the battle in March only eighteen could cover the eastern Atlantic and none at all covered the western half. All of the U.S. Navy's 112 VLR Liberators were in the Pacific, and all those of the USAAF were in Morocco for Operation Torch.

Aircraft still played a vital part, even on occasions when they did not launch an attack. U-boats tracked convoys on the surface, keeping a few miles away by day and sending radio signals to bring others into action. Then they attacked by night. To avoid aircraft they had to dive, and once submerged they were slow and blind, allowing the convoys to escape.

What had happened in less than two months that had turned a seemingly imminent Allied defeat into a triumph for the escort forces? There was no single reason. Instead, there were a combination of factors. Escort forces became stronger because the Allies temporarily stopped their convoys to Russia and reduced escort forces to North Africa. The Allied air forces began to send long-range aircraft to the North Atlantic. These aircraft and the escort carriers coming into service more or less closed the "air gap" where the U-boats had operated most successfully. Ultimately, Allied victories came from teamwork. This teamwork was expressed in the ease with which escort ships of different nationalities worked together. Allied scientists, industries, and commanders also cooperated well.

Sinking the *Scharnhorst*

While Dönitz struggled to find a new strategy for his U-boats, the second half of 1943 saw the end of the German navy's battleship force. On September 22, *Tirpitz* was crippled in its Norwegian base in a daring attack by British midget submarines. For the rest of its life the ship would be little more than a target for RAF bombers. A few days later *Lützow* left Norway

The German battleship *Scharnhorst*, at rest in port, saw action from 1939 to 1943. It was sunk by the British Home Fleet on December 26, 1943.

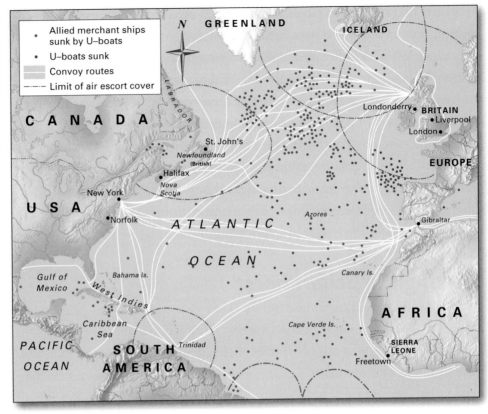

From March to September 1943, increased air escort cover helped the Allies close the "air gap," the area that was out of range of land-based air forces, where U-boats had operated successfully before.

for the Baltic to support the German land forces there. It would take no further part in the war's naval campaigns.

After these moves, *Scharnhorst* was the last large German ship able to strike into the Atlantic. After a long break the Allies re-started their convoys to Russia in November 1943. The first few convoys got through, but then Dönitz persuaded Hitler to let *Scharnhorst* see action. The main British Home Fleet was waiting. The commander in chief of the Home Fleet, Admiral Bruce Fraser, maneuvered his battleship *Duke of York* and its supporting forces to intercept *Scharnhorst*. On the evening of December 26, 1943, *Scharnhorst* was pounded into a wreck by gunfire and sunk by torpedoes. It was the end for Hitler's surface navy.

Despite this success and despite the outcome of the convoy battles fought in 1942 and 1943, the real turning points in the struggle took place in the shipyards. July 1942 is considered the month in which the Allies started

ESCORT CARRIERS

TECH

Before World War II the United States, Britain, and Japan all had aircraft carriers in service with their navies. These ships were too scarce and too valuable to use in everyday antisubmarine or convoy escort operations. However, wartime experience proved that naval air power on the spot was vital. Therefore, the U. S. and Britain built escort carriers to assist in the safety of the convoys.

The first escort carrier was the British *Audacity*. Built from a captured German banana boat, the escort carrier could hold only six planes. It entered service in the summer of 1941 but was sunk the following December. Despite its tiny air squadron, it proved its worth in its final convoy battle. The air squadron sunk five U-boats, and the convoy lost only two merchant ships.

When later escort carriers were built, each carried about twenty aircraft and they were made to order. In total, 130 escort carriers were built in American shipyards.

During the Battle of the Atlantic, the escort carriers served with the support groups that the Allies introduced to help threatened convoys from late 1942 onward. The escort carriers were crucial in hunting down and destroying the increasing number of U-boats. The escort carriers help ensure that Admiral Dönitz would not regain any initiative from the defeats the Germans suffered in the spring of 1943.

winning, for it was the first month since 1939 in which the quantity of new ships built was greater than losses. The second great milestone came in the early fall of 1943, when the total available Allied shipping stock rose above the level at the start of the war. The United States was now producing more ships in a single year than all the ships in existence in 1939. No longer was it possible for Germany to win the Battle of the Atlantic. Germany would also find it impossible to win the war.

▶ This B-17 Stratofortress, as seen in a fish-eye view, flies through the storms of war and above the chaos of fighting in Europe below.

3 The European Air War, 1942 to 1943

KEY PEOPLE	KEY PLACES	
🇬🇧 Air Chief Marshal Arthur Harris	卐 Lübeck, Germany	卐 Hamburg, Germany
🇺🇸 General Ira C. Eaker	卐 Cologne, Germany	卐 Berlin, Germany
🇬🇧 Winston Churchill	卐 Peenemünde, Germany	
卐 Adolf Hitler	🇲🇦 Casablanca, Morocco	

O n February 2, 1942, Air Chief Marshal Arthur Harris succeeded Air Chief Marshal Richard Peirse as commander in chief of RAF Bomber Command. Peirse left for a new command in India with the unjust burden of blame for errors in the Bomber Command offensive in 1941. After the offensive, an official inquiry found that while much had gone wrong, the key to future success was new technology. But the technology could only supplement the critical asset of the Bomber Command: dedicated crews.

On September 16, 1941, a prototype Avro Lancaster arrived for trials with No. 44 Squadron at its base. It was followed on December 24 by three Lancaster Mk Is. The nucleus of the RAF's first Lancaster squadron took shape. Four aircraft of No. 44 Squadron flew the Lancaster's first mission on March 3 to lay mines in the Heligoland Bight. The first night bombing mission came on March 10–11. Two Lancasters of the same squadron took part in an attack on Essen. In all, fifty-nine squadrons of Bomber Command used Lancasters during World War II. The aircraft gave the RAF a sharp edge in the air offensive against Germany.

The spring of 1942 also saw the introduction of the first of Bomber Command's long-awaited electronic aids: the TR 1335, known as "Gee." Pulses transmitted from stations in Britain were shown on a cathode-ray tube (CRT) in the aircraft. By measuring the time between each pulse, the navigator could fix the aircraft's position. He noted the point where the Gee coordinates intersected, converted the data and transferred it to a chart. Gee could also be used to bomb blind through clouds or of homing to base.

The spring of 1942 also saw the introduction of the first of Bomber Command's long-awaited electronic aids: the TR 1335, known as "Gee."

During 1941 much of Bomber Command's efforts were devoted to attacking the German battlecruisers *Scharnhorst and Gneisenau,* and the heavy cruiser *Prinz Eugen.* The escape of these warships through the English Channel on February 12, 1942 caused great embarrassment to the British. But it also meant that the command could once again give priority to the offensive against Germany's industry.

Bomber Command's New Directive

On February 14 a new directive was issued. It authorized Bomber Command to operate at maximum intensity wherever possible, without restriction. Great hopes were pinned on the use of Gee. It was thought that it would be several months before the enemy found a way to jam it. Targets were selected because they lay within range of Gee. The primary sites, chosen to undermine the morale of industrial workers, were Essen, Düsseldorf, Duisburg, and Cologne. Wilhelmshaven, Bremen, and Emden were selected as alternatives. Others outside the range of Gee—including Berlin—were added to the list for attack when conditions were favorable.

The British began what was called "area bombing"— attacking a large area, such as a city, instead of making precision attacks. After the war, Air Chief Marshal Arthur Harris was criticized for this tactic. In fact, the idea had originated in a directive to Bomber Command issued on October 25, 1940. The directive stressed that "if bombing is to have its full morale effect, it must on occasions produce heavy material destruction."

TARGET: WILHELMSHAVEN

On the morning of January 27, 1943, fifty-five B–17 bombers took off from English bases over the North Sea, in the first attack by U. S. bombers on a German target. They were headed for the naval base at Wilhelmshaven. At flying altitude the subzero temperatures cut through the crew's flight uniforms. Their machine guns, turrets, and camera mechanisms froze. The windshields and bombsights were obscured by layers of frost. A navigator for that attack described the outbound flight.

At about 10:30 the altimeter indicated 25,000 feet. The cloud cover had ended, far below, and we could see the surface of the sea—like a sheet of glass. At 10:45 the captain warned the crew to be extra alert. I looked out to the right and could see the outline of the coast of Germany and the row of islands that lay just off it. At 10:57 we were just over the islands, and at 11:00 the tail gunner reported flak at six o'clock, below. It was from the coastal islands and was the first time we were fired on from German soil. At this time we were beginning to turn and we crossed the island of Baltrum and went into German territory. As we turned, the bombardier elevated the muzzle of his gun and fired a burst so that the tracers arched over into Germany. The first shots from our plane, … but not the last!

Extract taken from *Storm from the Skies* by Robert Jackson. Arthur Barker, London, 1974.

A later directive made it clear that "the only target on which the night force could inflict effective damage was a whole German town."

Lübeck and the Baedecker Raids

The bombing directive was to remain unchanged for a year. In March they targeted Lübeck. This old German city was selected for a saturation attack with incendiaries instead of high explosives. Lübeck was considered a good target because many of its buildings were old and flammable and its streets narrow. This would create good conditions for the development of firestorms. The center of Lübeck, the *Altstadt*, was densely populated, with about 30,000 people. Another 90,000 lived in the suburbs.

On the night of March 28–29, 1942, 234 aircraft set out for Lübeck, Germany. The final wave, which was to attack an hour after the main force,

A total of 191 aircraft claimed to have hit their target, making the raid a complete success.

consisted of forty-seven Wellingtons and eighteen Manchesters with high explosives, including 4,000-lb. (1,812-kg) blast bombs. A total of 191 aircraft claimed to have hit their target, making the raid a complete success. Two hundred acres (81 hectares) of the city center were destroyed, mainly by fire. It took thirty-two hours for the last fires to be put out. About 1,000 dwellings were destroyed and 4,000 damaged; 320 civilians were killed and 785 injured. Eight bombers failed to return. The raid caused great panic in Lübeck and also within the German administration in Berlin. The Nazi leadership was quick to initiate reprisals, however.

These came in the form of "Baedecker" raids, named after the Baedecker tourist guides. Launched on the order of Adolf Hitler, they were directed against British towns and cities with historic and cultural importance. The first was carried out against Exeter on the night of April 23 and 24, 1942, by forty-five aircraft. This was followed by two raids against Bath on April 25 and 26. The city suffered heavily, and in three more raids Norwich was attacked twice and York once.

This map shows the major bombing raids carried out by the Germans and the British in 1942–1943.

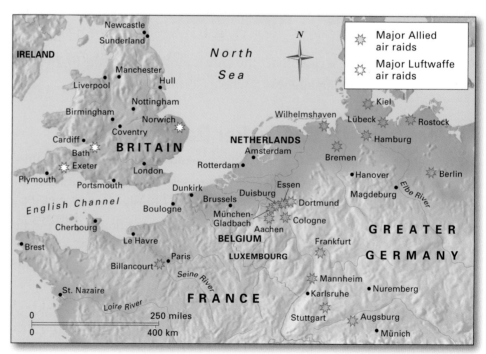

The most successful attack was on May 3–4, when Exeter was again targeted, this time with 131 tons of bombs. The downtown area of the city was severely damaged. During the rest of the month, Norwich, Hull, Canterbury, and other cities were attacked. The emphasis then switched to strategic targets such as Birmingham, Southampton, and Middlesbrough.

Meanwhile, the Allied attack on Lübeck had been followed by two heavy attacks on the Baltic port of Rostock and the Heinkel aircraft plant. In reporting the raids German radio announcers used for the first time the term *Terrorangriff* (terror attack). The attacks did not cause major worry. However, much worse was to come.

The attacks on Lübeck and Rostock produced the desired results, but that did not stop the Allies. On the night of May 30, 1942, Bomber Command flew 1,047 aircraft to Cologne. A total of 868 aircraft bombed the main target area, dropping 1,455 tons (1,319 tonnes) of bombs, two-thirds of which were incendiaries. The city suffered severe damage and a death toll of 469. Over 600 acres (243 hectares) of Cologne was destroyed. About 250 factories were ruined or badly damaged. Fifty percent of the city's power supply was cut. Gas and water supplies were disrupted. The railway repair shops, employing 2,500 people, were totally destroyed, and 12,000 fires started, some of which burned for several days. Bomber Command sustained a record loss of forty-one aircraft, of which twenty-nine were Wellingtons. Thirty-six were accounted for by German fighter planes.

German Air Defenses

The Cologne raid exposed problems with the German air defense system, the Kammhuber Line. This was made up of searchlights and antiaircraft guns, and a network of circular air defense zones (known as *Himmelbett*, or "fourposter bed" zones) along the North Sea coast. A further searchlight and antiaircraft (or flak) belt and nine more Himmelbett zones protected Berlin. Joint night-fighter and flak zones covered the industrial areas of the Ruhr.

The system was as rigorous as Kammhuber could make it, but each ground controller could still only direct a single fighter pilot, who then

STUDENTEN

SEID PROPA-GANDISTEN DES FÜHRERS

HOCH-u. FACHSCHULEN BEKENNEN SICH AM 29. MÄRZ ZUR DEUTSCHE FREIHEITSBEWEGUNG

relied on his vision to make contact with the target. As early as July 1939, the German communications firm Telefunken had shown the value of airborne interception radar equipment (AI) in air-to-air detection. The Luftwaffe Technical Office seemed to have no interest in the device, so Telefunken had developed it into a radar altimeter.

The AI concept was resurrected in the summer of 1940. The operational AI set was named Lichtenstein. It was early 1942 by the time Lichtenstein-equipped aircraft reached the *Nachtjagdgeschwader* (German night-fighter wings) in any number. Once they did, the effectiveness of the German night-fighter force increased greatly. Some pilots began to achieve remarkable scores. Unfortunately for Germany's cities, Kammhuber's efforts to expand and streamline the night air defense system, and the growing prowess of his pilots, were largely ignored by the Luftwaffe High Command.

Flying Fortresses in Europe

Early in 1942, while Bomber Command was developing its night offensive against Germany, the vanguard of the U.S. Eighth Army Air Force, commanded by General Ira C. Eaker, arrived in Britain. Much background work was needed: air bases had to be built, and a headquarters for the newly formed 8th Bomber Command was established at High Wycombe, northwest of London. On July 1 the first Flying Fortress to be used in the European theater, a Boeing B-17E of the 97th Bombardment Group, landed at Prestwick in Scotland.

On August 15, 1942, twenty-four crews of the 97th BG, from bases in East Anglia, were told to carry out the first American bombing attack

General Ira C. Eaker was the commander of the U.S. Eighth Air Force. Like his British counterpart Air Chief Marshal Arthur Harris, Eaker believed that strategic or "area" bombing undermined enemy morale.

from British soil. The Spitfire squadrons of No. 11 Group, RAF Fighter Command, provided fighter cover. After a delay, the mission took place on August 17. The target was the railroad yards at Rouen in France. Twelve B-17s took part, with six more flying a feint along the French coast. The bombing achieved good results, and only one B-17 received flak damage. On August 19, two B-17s (out of twenty-four sent out) bombed the German fighter airfield at Abbeville. All returned safely to base.

The buildup of B-17s in Britain, known as Operation Bolero, continued throughout the late summer of 1942. The second group to arrive, from August 9, 1942, was the 301st. Other bomber groups followed at different stages, and for the rest of the year the American daylight bombers carried out many attacks on targets in France and the Low Countries, all within range of fighter escort. Longer-range flights into Germany itself were delayed because of lack of long-range fighter escort aircraft and the Allied landings in North Africa.

At the beginning of January, 1943, Eaker judged that the time was right for the full-scale daylight offensive to begin. The objectives of that offen-

Allied bombers have hit a Nazi motor transport. The supplies lying scattered around the wreckage were ones that never reached the Germans.

sive, and that of the RAF Bomber Command, were set out. In January 1943, at a top-level conference, President Roosevelt, Prime Minister Winston Churchill, and the combined Allied Chiefs of Staff met in Casablanca, Morocco. One of the decisions was to combine the bombing arms of the Royal Air Force and United States Army Air Force into a single force. Its task would be "the progressive destruction and dislocation of the German military, industrial, and economic system, and the undermining of the morale of the German people to a point where their capacity for armed resistance is fatally weakened."

The Americans believed that they could best fulfill the demands of the Casablanca Directive by carrying out concentrated attacks on six principal target systems. These systems were submarine construction yards and bases, the aircraft industry, the ball-bearing industry, oil production, synthetic rubber production, and plants producing military transport.

The target of the first American raid on Germany was the naval base at Wilhelmshaven, a major center of U-boat production. The raid, on January 27, 1943, took the Germans by surprise. Fifty-three Flying Fortresses unloaded their bombs on Wilhelmshaven harbor, opposed by only a handful of Focke-Wulf 190s. Two more Fortresses bombed Emden. Only three B-17s failed to return. This gave hope that unescorted daylight operations could be successful. It would not be long before determined Luftwaffe fighter pilots shattered that myth.

Precision Bombing Operations

While the Americans built up their strategic bombing expertise in the early months of 1943, the RAF laid plans to carry out a daring and spectacular

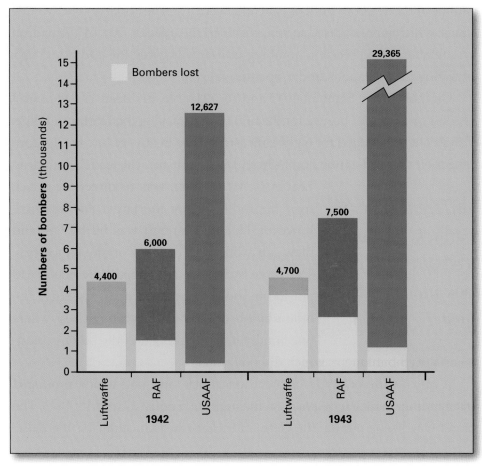

In 1942 and 1943, manufacture of U.S. aircraft soared, as American industrial capacity hit its peak. This graph demonstrates the production and losses among the U.S., British, and German air forces.

night attack on the great industrial dams of the Ruhr valley. Destruction of the dams, it was believed, would cause serious damage to the German war economy.

The attack was to be carried out by a new squadron, No. 617, using Lancasters modified to carry a special cylindrical mine. The mine weighed 9,250 pounds (4,190 kg), of which 6,600 pounds (2,989 kg) was a new and powerful explosive, RDX. The weapon was carried across the bomb bay of the Lancaster between two V-shaped arms. A mechanism caused the bomb to spin at 500 rpm, so that when it hit the reservoir behind the dam, it bounced across the surface until it struck the dam wall. It then bounced back and sank. Under the water its spin brought it back up against the wall. The explosive charge was set to detonate at a depth of 30 feet (9.15 m).

The attack took place on the night of May 16 and 17, 1943. Two dams, the Mohne and Eder, both built of concrete, were hit. The Sorpe and Schwelme dams, which were encased in soil, survived the attacks. No. 617 Squadron was retained as a precision bombing unit. It was given the additional task of testing new weapons under operational conditions.

On the night of September 15 and 16, 1943, No. 617 used 12,000-pound (5,436-kg) "Tallboy" bombs for the first time, attacking the Dortmund–Ems Canal. The plan called for eight Lancasters to go in at very low level, dropping their delayed-action bombs from 150 feet (46 m). The leader, Squadron Leader G. W. Holden, was to direct the attack over the radio. Before the target was reached, however, Holden's aircraft was hit by flak and blew up, followed by four more Lancasters. The three survivors continued, but one could not locate the target due to poor visibility. The others bombed the objective through heavy flak; one bomb fell in the canal and the other exploded on the embankment, which did not burst.

> *A much different type of precision attack, and one which produced outstanding results, took place on the night of August 17 and 18...*

A much different type of precision attack, and one which produced outstanding results, took place on the night of August 17 and 18, 1943. The target was Peenemünde, the German rocket-research center on the Baltic

PEENEMÜNDE: HITLER'S SECRET ROCKET BASE

TECH

In April 1936 the German Army Ordnance Board and the Air Ministry began turning the northern tip of the Baltic island of Peenemünde into a test center for rocket-powered weapons. Peenemünde became the largest of its kind of site in the world. The east section had test and manufacturing facilities for missiles that were to be used by the army. The west section was used by the Luftwaffe to test aircraft missiles and rocket-powered aircraft.

The two most important missiles tested at Peenemünde were the Fieseler Fi-103 (V-1) flying bomb, and the A-4 (V-2) rocket, which at that time flew higher and faster than anything else in the world. These weapons posed a terrible threat to the Allies beginning in the summer of 1944, when the first V-1s were launched from the French coast; 2,419 hit London and 2,448 hit Antwerp, Belgium. Similarly, 1,054 V-2s fell on Britain (517 on London) and 1,675 on targets in Europe, including 1,267 on Antwerp. The V-1 and V-2 both carried about a ton of explosives. Their damage would have been far more devastating had it not been for Allied air attacks on Peenemünde.

coast. A total of 597 heavy bombers were used in the attack, code-named Operation Hydra. The mission involved the precision bombing of a series of selected buildings grouped around three points. A new type of marker bomb was used. A 250-pound (113 kg) weapon was packed with cotton wool, which ignited at 3,000 feet (915 m). It burned with a brilliant crimson flame for about ten minutes.

The attack was highly successful, and Peenemünde suffered. As well as destroying vital sites and installations, the bombs killed 180 Germans. Many of them were leading scientists, setting back the German long-range rocket program by as much as six months. However, up to 600 foreign workers, mostly Poles, were also killed.

Area Raids on Hamburg

Contrasting with such precision attacks was the series of raids, code-named Operation Gomorrah, on Hamburg in July 1943. The first took place on the night of July 24 and 25. Seven hundred twenty-eight aircraft of Bomber

Command dropped 2,284 tons (2,072 tonnes) of bombs in fifty minutes, killing 1,500 people. Much of the success of this attack was attributed to the first use of "Window." These were strips of metal foil, cut to the wavelength of the enemy warning radar and dropped in bundles from the aircraft to confuse the defenses.

The following day Eighth Air Force B-17s made a daylight attack on the Blohm & Voss shipyards at Hamburg. On the night of July 27 and 28, 729 more aircraft of Bomber Command dropped 2,326 tons (2,110 tonnes) of bombs on working-class areas of Hamburg. About 40,000 people died in the firestorm that resulted. One million more people fled the city. The third attack on Hamburg was carried out by 707 aircraft on the night of July 29–30. A fourth attack, on August 2–3, was a failure because of thunderstorms. The whole series of attacks cost the RAF fifty-seven bombers, and the Americans nineteen.

As the summer of 1943 turned into fall, Bomber Command's night offensive crept toward Berlin. In September and early October, Mannheim and Kassel were heavily bombed. Two weeks later, on the night of November 18, Bomber Command struck the opening blow in the Battle of Berlin. The offensive, which lasted until March 24, 1944, saw sixteen major raids on Berlin. There were 9,111 sorties, most of which were made by Lancasters.

In this aerial photograph, bombs hurtle toward German targets. Allied raids on Hamburg dropped thousands of bombs in actions similar to this one.

The total cost to the RAF was ninety-two aircraft destroyed over enemy territory and 954 damaged.

American Losses

It was not until the spring of 1944, when long-range fighter escorts became available, that the Americans were able to successfully help Britain in the Battle of Berlin. There were several reasons.

August 1943 was a bad month. On August 1, 179 Liberators were dispatched from North African bases to attack oil refineries at Ploesti, Romania. These refineries supplied much of Germany's fuel. One aircraft crashed on takeoff, eleven more turned back for various reasons, and the B-24 carrying the lead navigator was lost. The bombers were heavily engaged by antiaircraft batteries over the target and suffered severe fighter attacks. The target was left in flames. But the damage was not as great as had been hoped. The cost to the Ninth Air Force was fifty-three Liberators and 440 aircrew killed or missing, with 200 more taken prisoner after bailing out.

The bombers were heavily engaged by antiaircraft batteries over the target and suffered severe fighter attacks.

Then came the "Anniversary Raids" of August 17, 1943. This time, 376 B-17s were sent to attack ball-bearing factories at Schweinfurt and the Messerschmitt assembly plant at Regensburg. It was the deepest penetration mission so far by the USAAF. Both targets were hit, but sixty bombers were shot down and many more were badly damaged. On October 14, 291 B-17s set out to attack Schweinfurt again. No fewer than seventy-seven failed to return, and 133 more were damaged. That day, "Black Thursday," was the low point of a week in which the Eighth Air Force lost 148 heavy bombers and nearly 1,500 airmen.

However, a new USAAF fighter group, the 354th, was arriving at Boxted Air Base in the southeast of England. By December the group would be ready to fly its first escort mission. The aircraft it flew was the North American P-51 Mustang. This was a fast, long-range fighter. In just a few months, it would help turn the tide of the air war over Europe.

German Chancellor Adolf Hitler addresses 1,500,000 Nazi Germans on National Labor Day, May 1, 1935. The assembly has marched to the Tempelhof Airport in Berlin, Germany, to hear Hitler's May Day address.

4 Control, Persecution, and the Holocaust: the Nazi State, 1936 to 1945

KEY PEOPLE	KEY PLACES	
Heinrich Himmler	Auschwitz-Birkenau	Chelmno
Reinhard Heydrich	Belzec	Majdenek
Albert Speer	Sobibor	
Adolf Hitler	Treblink	

Using strategies ranging from the cult of personality to systematic genocide, Hitler brought civilians in Germany and wartime occupied Europe to their knees before the all-powerful Nazi State. Hitler consolidated his position as dictator of Nazi Germany by eliminating rivals within the Nazi Party. As Hitler dominated the Nazi Party, the Nazis dominated German society through both cooperation and force.

To many Germans in the 1930s the Nazi regime helped lower unemployment, boost economic recovery, and bring social and political order. Opposition to the state was minimal. Any oppositotion to Nazi power was almost always rooted out and destroyed. Apart from a few brave individuals, Germans who had trouble with Nazism kept quiet, since public dissent led to death.

At the very center of Hitler's view of the world was the concept of racial struggle. Hitler and the Nazis argued that Germans were the natural masters of Europe of other, lesser races. This "philosophy" included the strict control of the German people and the brutal treatment of others. In the case of the Jews and the Sinti and Roma peoples (Gypsies), Nazis made efforts to remove them from the face of the Earth.

The Mechanisms of State Control

Heinrich Himmler was the individual responsible for overseeing the control over the German people, and later German-occupied Europe. A fanatical Nazi, Himmler took charge of Hitler's personal protection squad, the *Schutzstaffel* (SS), in 1929. He rapidly expanded its operations. Himmler wished to create an Aryan brotherhood of political soldiers devoted to Hitler and the Nazi cause.

Adolf Hiter was an electrifying speaker. He inspired fanatic devotion from some Germans, such as Henirich Himmler, the Head of the German Police (the SS).

The SS began to gain control of the German police force and intelligence services. This move was completed by June 17, 1936, when Himmler took on the title "Reichsführer-SS and Head of the German Police." In the summer of 1934 the SS took control of the concentration camp system. The SS enlarged the system during the 1930s, making the camps places to hold "undesirables" and opponents of the Nazis.

Originally set up as work camps, the concentration camps later became the scenes of industrialized slaughter. A military formation was set up to guard the camps.

These *SS-Totenkopfverbände* (SS Death's-Head Units), along with the Hitler's own guard, the *Leibstandarte Adolf Hitler*, became the nucleus of the *Waffen Schutzstaffel* (armed SS). Following the outbreak of war in 1939,

HEINRICH HIMMLER

KEY FIGURES

Heinrich Himmler (1900–1945) was an officer cadet who did not see service in World War I. He joined the Nazi Party in 1925.

Four years later, he became chief of the SS. During the 1930s he gained sole control of the police and security services, which were absorbed into the SS. He assumed charge of the growing concentration camp system. During the war he was made Racial Commissioner for the Strengthening of German Nationhood. This post gave him great powers in the eastern territories. The 1944 July bomb plot, led by German army officers, further strengthened Himmler's position. Himmler was appointed chief of the Replacement Army. Despite lacking any military experience, he was even briefly given command of Army Group Vistula on the eastern front.

After the German surrender Himmler tried to escape in disguise, but was captured. He committed suicide by taking poison on May 23, 1945. Himmler looked more like a bank clerk than a ruthless killer. But he was a bureaucrat obsessed by the concept of racial superiority, prepared to sacrifice millions to that aim.

Heinrich Himmler

the Waffen-SS expanded from just 23,000 men to over 800,000 troops in thirty-eight divisions. From late 1944 onward, the Waffen-SS would even threaten the power of the German army.

During the war the SS set up economic programs. These used the inmates of the concentration camps as a source of cheap labor. Gradually the SS became so large and powerful that historians have called it a "dual state" or a "state within a state." As the war progressed, Hitler became disenchanted with the regular organizations of the German state, especially the army. He looked to the SS for support—which Himmler was happy to provide.

The heart of the SS was its police and intelligence services. The German police made itself above the law. For example, with a *Schutzhaftbefehl* (Order for Protective Custody), policemen were able to arrest and detain people at will. Throughout Nazi Germany there was competition between old German institutions and those of the Nazi Party. This resulted in confusion and inefficiency. One area, however, where such chaos did not reign was within the SS police and intelligence services.

THE NIGHT OF LONG KNIVES

KEY EVENTS

The rowdiest and most undisciplined of Hitler's forces were the SA Storm Troopers. At their head was the radical, nonconformist, and tough war veteran Ernst Röhm. The SA troopers and Röhm sympathized with the radical, left wing of the Nationalist Socialist German Worker's Party (Nazi Party). They shocked Hitler with their beliefs. Reportedly, in the power struggle, Röhm called Hitler a swine who had sold out the party for an alliance with the conservative establishment and the army.

During the night of January 29–30, 1934, the SS, Göring's police, and Röhm's other personal enemies of Himmler and Goebbels struck. Röhm and the entire leadership of the SA were taken to Stadelheim prison in Munich. Röhm refused to shoot himself. He told the guards that Hitler could come to his cell and do his own dirty work. At that, Röhm was shot by the SS. Hitler took this opportunity to murder other former political allies. Hitler later admitted to only seventy-seven executions. However in Berlin, 150 SA leaders were shot. The total number of victims will never be known.

Under the leadership of Reinhard Heydrich, the police were reorganized. In 1936 Heydrich was given command of the Sipo (*Sicherheitspolizei* or security police), which was a combination of the Kripo (*Kriminalpolizei* or criminal investigation police) and the Gestapo (*Geheime Staatspolizei* or state secret police). In 1939 Heydrich was also appointed head of the RSHA (*Reichssicherheitshauptamt* or Reich Security Main Office).

The RSHA was responsible for three key functions. One was the suppression of anti-Nazi elements within Germany and occupied Europe. Second, the RSHA was in charge of intelligence gathering at home and abroad. Third, it was charged with the elimination of racial undesirables. Within Germany the agencies of the RHSA received cooperation from the general public. In the occupied territories they got support from the German armed forces. Individuals or groups who agreed to work for the Germans against their own people also assisted.

The sudden conquests of large areas of Europe from 1939 to 1941 enlarged the scope of the RHSA. In each occupied territory a central police and intelligence office was established. Regional SS departments were set up under them. The SS was able to act against the local populations. In the east it was actively encouraged to exterminate Jews and Communists and their supporters. The feared *Einsatzgruppen* were used to terrible effect in the 1939 Polish campaign. Their function was to eliminate Jews and Polish intellectuals. The Einsatzgruppen would later be used during the invasion of the Soviet Union in 1941. In the space of little over six months they murdered more than half a million people.

> *In most cases, the Gestapo relied upon informers to denounce their own neighbors.*

In the years following World War II the Gestapo gained a reputation for ruthless efficiency. In Germany, however, its presence and range of operations were limited. In most cases, the Gestapo relied upon informers to denounce their own neighbors. The Gestapo's numbers were also surprisingly small. In the Würzburg region—an area of 1 million people—there were only twenty-eight Gestapo officials. Of these, nearly half were involved in administrative duties.

ENACTING THE WILL OF THE FÜHRER

A common Nazi slogan was: "The will of the Führer is law!" But what exactly was the will of the Führer? Hitler, outside of the military, issued few orders or directives. In the strange world of Nazi government, officials and administrators tried to anticipate Hitler's orders.

A leading Third Reich historian, Professor Ian Kershaw, has called this attempt to carry out Hitler's wishes "working toward the Führer" after a speech by a Nazi official, Werner Willikens, gave a speech in 1934. Willikens stated that it was the duty of all good Nazis to guess Hitler's intentions. "Anyone who makes mistakes," warned Willikens, "will notice it soon enough. But anyone who really works toward the Führer ... will in the future have the finest reward in the form of the sudden legal confirmation of his work."

So Hitler would outline his broad aims, leaving it to those beneath him to sort out the details and make things happen. As a political gambler, Hitler always preferred radical or extreme solutions to a problem. This encouraged his subordinates to look for radical solutions, whether in military matters—such as the offensive through the Ardennes in 1944—or in the extermination of the Jews.

As a consequence, the Gestapo's main function was to sort through the mass of denunciations that came its way rather than to actively seek out the troublemakers.

Secret denunciations became something of a way of life in Nazi Germany. The authorities actively encouraged people to spy on their neighbors, to track down fare beaters on the public transport system, to keep tabs on former socialists or, in the 1940s, to root out Jews hiding within the community.

Denunciations were used for many different reasons: to settle old scores, or get rid of a business rivals (in the 1930s denunciations were ways for Germans to elbow aside rival Jewish businesses). Other motivations included romance. In one instance, a wife who had found a new love interest, arranged for the police to eavesdrop on her husband. The police overheard him expressing anti-Nazi comments. The wife received a divorce and her husband a four-year jail sentence. Denunciations also gave the downtrodden a chance for revenge on their economic and social superiors. As historian Richard Grunberger puts it, the system of informing "harnessed a vast reservoir of personal resentment and spite to the purposes of the state."

Daily Life under the Nazis

The key Nazi belief about how German people should live was based on blood and race. A new united community would be created, the *Volksgemeinschaft* (folk community). The Nazis insisted the community be made up of physically healthy people of Aryan stock. They needed to be committed to the ideals of the Nazi regime. All others were to be excluded. The Nazi transformation of German society did not require the creation of new social and economic structures, as in Communist Soviet Union. It required the German people to change the way they thought about themselves. And even though the Nazi Volksgemeinschaft was never fully realized, the practice did set the pattern for much Nazi policy. Within this "folk community" the German people were expected to commit themselves to the state. Children were required to join youth organizations, such as the Hitler Youth or the League of German Maidens. Adults were encouraged to join the Nazi Party or to become part of groups such as the SA. Independent thought and displays of unusual behavior were discouraged.

EYEWITNESS

MARIA KRAUS

This Gestapo record reveals how dangerous it was for anyone to step out of line in Nazi Germany. Ilse Totzke was one such person. Her Jewish sympathies landed her in the Ravensbrück concentration camp. But she only came to the attention of the Gestapo because of a denunciation by a neighbor, Maria Kraus, in 1940.

Ilse Totzke is a resident next door to us. I noticed her because she is of Jewish appearance. I should like to mention that Miss Totzke never responds to the German greeting [the Heil Hitler salute]. I gathered from what she was saying that her attitude was always anti-German. On the contrary she always favored France and the Jews. Among other things, she told me the German army was not as well equipped as the French. Now and then a woman of about 36 years comes and she is of Jewish appearance. To my mind Miss Totzke is behaving suspiciously. I thought she might be engaged in some kind of activity which is harmful to the German Reich.

The Nazis exploited the concept of "enforced consensus." Individuals were strongly encouraged to show their "spontaneous" enthusiasm for the Nazi cause. The *Heil Hitler* salute, which the Nazis called "the German greeting," became just one way of showing enthusiasm. Not to reply in the same manner implied an anti-German outlook. And to fail to display a swastika flag during a Nazi parade was seen as unpatriotic. Such actions could bring about a Gestapo investigation.

Volksgemeinschaft extended to helping the poor in a highly regimented manner. For example, "one-pot meals" were held one Sunday a month. The money saved went into the *Winterhilfe* (Winter Relief) program. Winter Relief was a major Nazi charity, and party helpers bombarded people for

This propaganda poster encourages people to support the Nazi organization.

DAS VOLK — WÄHLT LISTE — 1 — NATIONALSOZIALISTEN — Reichstagswahl 6.11.32

donations. In contrast to other programs devised by the Nazis, Winter Relief worked. Nearly 9 million people received benefits in 1938.

Germans were aware of the dark side of the Nazi regime, but they did not want to get involved. Although the regime limited people's freedom, most considered this an acceptable price to pay for order. Nazism had swept away the old class-based political parties of the 1920s and overturned the humiliations of the Versailles treaty. By the late 1930s the Nazis could boast that Germany was once again a major world power. It had a growing economy. Its armed forces were the envy of the world.

The outbreak of war in 1939 worried the German people. Memories of 1914 to 1918 were still in many minds.

The outbreak of war in 1939 worried the German people. Memories of 1914 to 1918 were still in many minds. But the easy victories of 1939 to 1941 reassured many that the Führer was right once again. The war brought further limitations on personal freedom: moves were restricted; people had to show their passes more often; the police got involved in personal matters. On the economic side, however, the Nazis ensured that food supplies were plentiful. For many, the early years of the war brought increased wealth. Exchange rates in the conquered countries were set to favor Germany. Soldiers sent and brought home luxury goods from the occupied territories, such as furs from Norway, dairy products from Holland, silks and perfume from Paris. Oblivious to the sufferings of the people of Europe, the Germans enjoyed the fruits of the Wehrmacht's victories.

Even when the tide of war turned against the Axis powers in 1943, the German people continued to support the Nazi government. To the surprise of the SS, who secretly monitored German public opinion, morale held firm. The constant bombing of German cities, the threat of invasion from the Soviet Union, and the Allied demand for "unconditional surrender" seemed to stiffen the resolve of the people.

It was only toward the end of 1944 that the social order began to break down. This included the looting of bombed-out houses and the raiding of food supplies. The SS and Gestapo then adopted new measures to make public examples of those they called *Volksschädling,* enemies of the people. In October 1944, for example, seventeen post-office workers in Vienna were caught taking chocolate and soap from army food parcels. The accused were marched to an open square and publicly executed. In the final months of the war, other, similar minor crimes were also punished with death.

In the final stages of the war, the German people learned the true nature of the Nazi regime. But for the peoples of occupied Europe the Nazi nature had been present since the conquest of their countries. In Germany's New Order the occupied territories served the interests of the Reich. How conquered nations fared depended on a number of factors.

In the final stages of the war, the German people learned the true nature of the Nazi regime.

Their position on the Nazi ladder of racial superiority and the form of government imposed upon them by the Nazis were two of them.

At the top of the racial pile were the Norwegians, Dutch, and Danes. They were considered fellow Aryans who had failed to come over to the Nazi cause. The French and most of the Belgians were seen as earning German loathing through the imposition of the Versailles Treaty. The chief targets of Nazi racial hatred were the Slavic peoples of the east, especially Poland and Russia. Yet even they ranked one notch above the people the Nazis thought to be subhuman: the Jews. The Nazis maintained that it was no coincidence that most European Jewry was to be found in Poland and the Soviet Union.

As the war turned against Germany, the authorities clamped down on the civilian populations of Europe. They removed foodstuffs and other basic materials as well as manpower. In the east, civilians lived on the verge of starvation. Not until the winter of 1944 did those in occupied western Europe began to suffer the same fate. Despite the fact that Holland has the most fertile land in Europe, its people suffered particularly badly. During the winter of 1944–1945 the Dutch were reduced to eating sugar beets and tulip bulbs, and 16,000 died of starvation.

Any signs of resistance were crushed by the Nazi authorities. One of the central features of German policy in the occupied territories was collective responsibility. Any act of resistance would cause the whole civilian population to suffer as a result. Hostages were routinely taken. For example, if a German soldier was killed then ten or twenty hostages would be shot in response. Larger acts of resistance were met by correspondingly larger acts of retaliation. It might include the destruction of an entire village and the killing of its inhabitants.

Forced Labor

German economists had long known that a war economy would need more manpower than Germany could provide. Their answer was to use forced labor from the countries Germany had conquered. Although many did not wish to allow Slavs into the Reich, the numbers of Polish POWs (prisoners

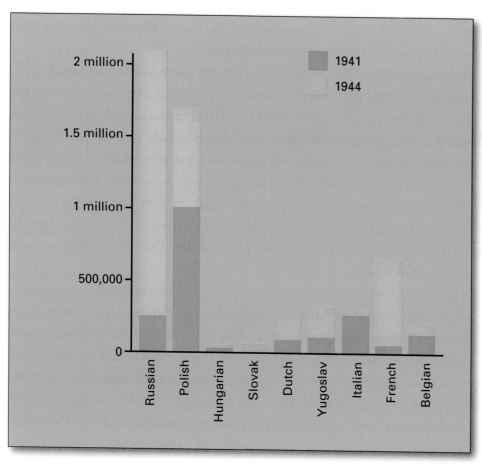

Between 1941 and 1944, foreign workers contributed to the labor force in the German Reich. Most of the workers were forced laborers, engaged in heavy industry, mining, and in the manufacture of arms.

of war) captured in 1939 were too large to ignore. This force was added to by Polish civilians rounded up by the Nazis. A total of over 1.4 million Poles were forced to work in the Reich.

The fall of France in 1940 supplied the next pool of labor. French POWs provided the bulk of a work force that would rise to nearly 1 million people. The invasion of the Soviet Union in 1941 provided even more manpower, but Nazi hatred of Russians ensured that many POWs were killed before they could be forced to work. It was only in the spring of 1942 that attitudes began to change. Under the leadership of Fritz Sauckel more than 2.5 million Soviet citizens were deported to Germany.

By 1944 the number of foreigners working in Germany had risen to over 7 million.

By 1944 the number of foreigners working in Germany had risen to over 7 million. Even this was not enough to support the demands of the German war economy. German planners then looked toward the SS-run concentration camps.

Since 1938 the SS had used concentration-camp inmates to run its quarries, brickworks, and repair facilities. As the numbers in the camps expanded (from about 25,000 in 1939 to 700,000 in January 1945) it was clear that this was an underutilized source of labor. Late in 1942 Albert Speer, the minister for armaments and munitions, made a decision. He insisted that the SS release concentration camp inmates to work in German factories. Many worked on special underground projects, such as the tunnels for the construction of V-weapons. Conditions were horrendous. Many of the slave laborers were literally worked to death. Their life expectancy was measured in months.

Initially, Jews did not form part of this new concentration camp workforce. From 1942, their fate was deemed to be extermination. However, the Germans began to employ small numbers, notably in the construction of the IG Farben works at Auschwitz. With the acute shortage of manpower from 1944 onward, increasing numbers of Jews were diverted from the gas chambers to work as slave laborers. At the end of 1944 roughly 600,000 concentration camp inmates (Jewish and non-Jewish) were listed for employment. But only 480,000 were considered fit for work.

ANNE FRANK

Anne Frank (1929-1945) was the daughter of German-Jewish businessman Otto Frank. The family had fled to Amsterdam in 1933 to avoid Nazi persecution. After invading Holland in 1940, the Nazis enacted anti-Jewish measures. In July 1942, the Frank family was forced into hiding.

The Franks spent the next two years secretly living in a few rooms above a warehouse office in the center of Amsterdam. It was here that Anne kept the diary that was to make her internationally famous.

The diary is a day-to-day account of the hardships endured by the family. The diary is written with honesty, humor, and optimism. Anne and her family avoided detection until August 4, 1944, when the family was betrayed to the Gestapo. The Franks were sent to concentration camps. Anne died in Bergen-Belsen in March 1945. Only Otto Frank survived the war.

Rounding up Europe's Jews

When Hitler came to power in 1933, just over half a million Jews lived in Germany. Almost immediately the Nazis began to eliminate the Jewish population. SA troops threatened and beat them. Jews could not marry non-Jews. They were removed from their professions and forced to hand over their businesses to non-Jews. Before the outbreak of war Jews were actively encouraged to emigrate from Germany, and around half of them did so. A few, sent to the newly established concentration camps, joined Communists, socialists, homosexuals, and others thought to be anti-German.

The transformation and hardening of Nazi attitudes toward the Jews came after the German victory over Poland. Approximately 2.5 million Jews came under Nazi control. Polish Jews were even more despised than their German counterparts. The Germans decided to force Poland's Jews into small enclaves, or ghettos. There, their numbers would waste away through overwork, starvation, cold, and disease.

German conquests in Scandinavia, western Europe, and the Balkans during 1940–1941 brought more Jews under Nazi control. The next great transformation in attitudes toward the Jews came with the invasion of the Soviet Union in June 1941. It marked the beginning of the *Endlösung* (Final Solution)—when the so-called "Jewish question" was to be resolved by the extermination of all Europe's Jews.

The Final Solution was confirmed by the Nazis at the Wannsee Conference of January 20. By then the rounding up and deportation of Jews to concentration camps was already happening. The percentage of Jewish deaths to prewar national populations varied considerably across Europe. In certain countries the local people helped the Germans either to kill Jews or deport them to the death camps.

> *In certain countries the local people helped the Germans either to kill Jews or deport them to the death camps.*

In eastern Europe Lithuanians, Ukrainians, and Romanians helped destroy their large Jewish populations. In France there was cooperation by the Vichy authorities in the rounding up of Jews.

But at the same time many Jews were hidden by locals. In Holland 106,000 Dutch Jews from a total population of 140,000 were sent to their deaths. Still, attempts were made by the Dutch to prevent Jewish depor-

THE WANNSEE CONFERENCE

KEY EVENTS

In July 1941 Hermann Göring ordered Reinhard Heydrich, chief of the SS RSHA, to draw up plans for "a final solution to the Jewish question." Many Nazi authorities were consulted as to how this might be done. On January 20, 1942, a conference, attended by fifteen leading Nazis, was held in a secluded house in the Berlin suburb of Grossen-Wannsee.

Under Heydrich's chairmanship, the conference approved the Nazi decision to end all attempts to expel Jews through emigration. Instead, they would send them to Poland. There the weak would die in transit or through overwork. The remainder would be exterminated in death camps.

The meeting was held under great secrecy, and the discussion was deliberately written in hazy language. The overall program was designated the "Final Solution." The deaths from starvation and overwork were "natural diminution." Those Jews remaining were to be "treated accordingly"—that is, murdered. The calm discussions of a group of Nazi bureaucrats confirmed a death sentence upon Europe's Jews.

ORADOUR-SUR-GLANE

In eastern Europe, destruction of whole villages by the German armed forces was so commonplace that they almost went unnoticed. In western Europe, however, such massacres were less common, and they were better documented.

In the summer of 1944, in retaliation to attacks from the French resistance on the 2nd SS Panzer Division Das Reich, a motorized SS infantry unit peeled off from their line of march. They arrived by chance in the small village of Oradour-sur-Glane, near the town of Limoges. The Germans rounded up all the inhabitants they could find. They forced the women and children into the local church. They put the men into five outlying barns. Then the Gemans set all six buildings ablaze. Anyone attempting to escape was shot. Altogether, 642 men, women, and children died in the slaughter. The village was never rebuilt and stands today, still gutted from the fires, as an example of Nazi war crimes.

tations. Elsewhere in Europe the Nazis were less successful at deporting Jews. In Denmark almost all of the country's 5,500 Jews were removed to safety in neutral Sweden. Bulgaria refused to hand over its 50,000 Jews. Following the deportation of fifteen Jews, Finland refused to hand over its remaining 2,000 Jews. In Hungary the government held back its large Jewish population until the Germans occupied it in March 1944. As a result, 200,000 Hungarian Jews were killed at Auschwitz–Birkenau. Still 300,000 managed to escape through Hungarian resistance to Nazi demands. Italy initially resisted, but after the German occupation of 1943 up to 15 percent of the country's Jews were deported.

In Hungary the government held back its large Jewish population until the Germans occupied it in March 1944.

The Death Camps

When the Germans began to exterminate all Jews in occupied Europe, the practice marked a change in Nazi policy. Before, the killing of Jews in the street and deaths caused by maltreatment were almost casual.

But now, Jews were to be sought out for death. Like the Jews, the Sinti and Roma peoples were considered as a race fit only for extermination. Most of them lived in eastern Europe and the Balkans.

The Einsatzgruppen had killed vast numbers of Jews. But it was decided that the most efficient extermination method was to send Jews to extermination camps. There they would be murdered using poison gas. Situated in Poland, the first three camps were Belzec, Sobibor, and Treblinka.

These camps began operations in March 1942. They were joined by Chelmno, Majdenek, and the Auschwitz–Birkenau complex. (Auschwitz-Birkenau was both a death and work camp. Its notoriety came largely because relatively high numbers of labor camp prisoners survived to tell their stories).

EINSATZGRUPPEN

STRATEGY & TACTICS

Einsatzgruppen (task forces) were mobile killing squads employed by the Nazis to eliminate opponents. First tried in Austria in 1938, Einsatzgruppen were used in the 1939 Polish campaign. Their main role was the elimination of the Polish elites—army officers, priests, intelligentsia—and the random killing of Jews or rounding them up into ghettos.

During the invasion of the Soviet Union in 1941, Einsatzgruppen were used more widely. There were about 3,000 of them, organized into five columns. They were ordered to kill any Jews and Communist officials they met. They called upon army units and local people to assist them. By the end of November 1941 at least 500,000 Jews may have been killed by Einsatzgruppen. The final death total may be as high as 2 million.

In each town or village on an Einsatzgruppen "death list," Jews and any other "undesirables" would be rounded up, marched to a secluded spot, and be made to dig a large pit. The victims were robbed of any valuables and then shot. Their bodies were thrown into the pit, which was hastily covered up.

In Lithuania a local villager recalled witnessing one such massacre by fellow Lithuanians under Einsatzgruppen supervision: "The women, children and old men were shot inside the pit. The children were going from person to person, shouting 'Mummy, Daddy, Mummy, Daddy, Mummy!' I think someone was calling for his daughter. And along came a really fat man with a pistol and bang, bang! All the grief and weeping was just heartbreaking. Even now, I cannot bear the lamenting and crying there."

The concentration camps had rows of barrack huts for both prisoners and guards as well as workshops, factories, or quarries. The death camps in contrast were relatively small and simple. Treblinka, a camp in which between 800,000 and 1 million people were killed, was only 450 by 700 yards (415 x 650 m) large. It was run by a staff of just fifty Germans and 150 Ukrainians, plus 1,000 Jews were to help sort out the bodies and their personal effects.

The Nazis established concentration and extermination camps. Following the Wannsee Conference in January 1942, camps for the sole purpose of mass murder were set up in eastern Europe (*shown in black*). Gas chambers were added to some of the existing concentration or work camps elsewhere in the Reich (*shown in gray*).

Barbed wire surrounds the horrible activities that took place inside the Auschwitz-Birkenau concentration camp.

The operation of a death camp like Treblinka consisted of phases of killing. It began with the arrival of a trainload of Jews—a railroad station was situated near the camp. The prisoners would be herded off the train to a central square, where the men and women were separated. Both men and women would then be forced to strip, and their clothes and other valuables were taken to a sorting area. The women also had their heads shaved, the hair being used to stuff mattresses. The naked prisoners were then marched to a shower block, which, unknown to them, was actually a gas chamber. Once inside the "shower block," the doors were bolted and the gas turned on. After the gas had taken effect, the corpses were dragged out by the Jewish guards and thrown into a mass grave pit. Some were burned in specially constructed ovens. The entire process would take a few hours at most.

This stack of prisoners' clothing in a German concentration camp stands in mute testimony to the crimes against humanity that took place inside the camp.

The death camps proved highly effective: the vast majority of Jews in eastern Europe were killed in 1942–1943. This was followed by Jews from western Europe and then from Hungary. By 1945 between 5.3 and 5.9 million Jews had been killed by the Nazis, as well as an estimated 500,000 homosexuals and 250,000 Sinti and Roma.

Hitler never achieved his aim of eliminating all Jews from Europe. But he did succeed in destroying the Jewish heartland of central and eastern Europe. It is a baleful legacy that continues to haunt Europe to this day.

▶ Grain from the Ukraine provided Germany with food from 1940 on, following a Nazi-Soviet agreement.

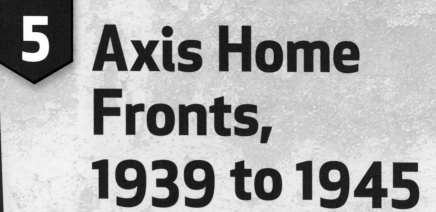

5 Axis Home Fronts, 1939 to 1945

KEY PEOPLE		KEY PLACES
Adolf Hitler	Hideki Tojo	Germany
Joseph Goebbels	Helmuth von Moltke	Italy
Benito Mussolini		Japan

World War II was a total war—a conflict in which civilians were strategic targets. When the United States and Britain bombed German cities during 1942, their target was neither industry nor key government and communications facilities. Instead, as a Bomber Command directive put it, it was the "morale of the enemy civil population and in particular [that] of the industrial workers."

Total war also meant directing all industry and business toward the war effort. The Axis powers proved less capable than the Allies in doing so. The people in the Axis countries were also less able to maintain enthusiasm for the war effort. As the fighting continued amid prospects of an Allied victory and a worsening economy, it became harder and harder for people living in the Axis countries to keep up their morale.

The harsh deprivations of war steadily eroded any beliefs of the people of Germany, Italy, and Japan that their leaders would achieve the promised swift victory.

Germany—Butter or Guns

"We have no butter, my countrymen, but I ask you—would you rather have butter or guns?" The question was posed by Hermann Göring in 1936, when the effects of the Depression were still being felt. Göring concluded: "Preparedness makes us powerful. Butter merely makes us fat."

One of the important results of the Nazi–Soviet pact of 1939 was economic cooperation. This agreement allowed Hitler to beat the British blockade.

Germany entered the war with good reserves of oil, coal, and rubber. One of the important results of the Nazi–Soviet pact of 1939 was economic cooperation. This agreement allowed Hitler to beat the British blockade. Raw materials and food were imported from and through the USSR from Romania, Iran, Afghanistan, and East Asia. Early in 1940, Soviet leader Joseph Stalin made an agreement with Nazi Germany. After sending arms and machinery to the Soviet Union, Germany in return would receive millions of tons of grains and gasoline, and large amounts of iron ore and other minerals from the Soviet Union.

From 1938 to 1944, German military expenditures increased by 500 percent. However, even this level of spending could not match the amount that the Allies, particularly the United States, were able to pour into the war effort.

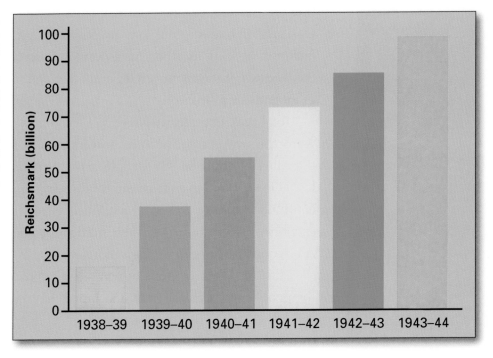

When World War II began, most foreign governments believed that Germany was ahead of them in military preparedness, and in putting its economy on a war footing. They were misled. Hitler, despite Göring's talk, was worried that lowering living standards or cutting the production of consumer goods would anger the Germans. He counted on a swift victory. For a year or two Blitzkrieg did the job.

From the very beginning of the conflict the British government understood the importance of putting the economy on a war footing. Production for the war effort took top priority in economic planning. The Nazis, too, had plans for the control of production, employment, and wages. However, the government did almost nothing to change how the German economy worked.

The Nazis, too, had plans for the control of production, employment, and wages.

Part of the trouble was the chaos at the heart of Hitler's dictatorship. Chains of command and rational planning were almost impossible to put in place when everything depended upon the whim of the Führer. With one or two exceptions, Germany's top businessmen were not brought in to discuss rearmament and its place in industry.

Hitler always placed a higher emphasis on political goals than economic ones. He believed that an Aryan woman's place was in the home, raising a family. So, putting German women to work in arms factories, as the British were doing, was not a viable option. In terms of Nazi ideology, this shift in worker gender could endanger the supremacy of the Aryan race. Between 1939 and the end of the war, the number of German women at work rose by only a few hundred thousand. The male labor force, depleted by the call-up of skilled workers into the armed forces, decreased by about 50 percent.

The Nazi government was awakened by the Soviet gains of late 1941 and early 1942. Clearly, victory was a long way off. In 1942 Hitler appointed Albert Speer to take control of arms production. Germany by then was able to exploit the raw materials of Nazi-occupied countries and to use foreign men and women in the occupied zones as forced labor.

JOSEPH GOEBBELS AND NAZI PROPAGANDA

The most impressive passages in *Mein Kampf* contain Hitler's analysis of the power of propaganda and the techniques used to make it effective. He understood that for propaganda to work a mass audience had to be saturated with it. He also understood that truth and falsehood were of small importance. What mattered was repeating a few ideas, in formulas, over and over again. The man to whom he entrusted Nazi propaganda was Joseph Goebbels.

Goebbels repaid Hitler's trust. Week after week, year after year, he reminded the people of Germany that in Hitler they had an ideal leader. Hitler was a man sent to them by Providence, a man in whom the ideals of the German race found their representation, and a man worthy of adulation. Of course, the message was received only because people were willing to receive it.

Goebbels also had a shrewd sense of the theatrical. His talent was put to good effect on the night of January 30, 1933, when Hitler became the chancellor of Germany. A torchlight procession streamed for hours past the Chancellery. Their zeal was evident in the glowing faces of the swastika-brandishing SA fanatics, their arms outstretched in the Nazi salute. As cries of "Heil Hitler" broke against the crisp winter air, Germany seemed to have more than a new chancellor. Not just political change, this event symbolized the dawning of a new age.

Goebbels was the first person to use video as a propaganda tool disgustingly in a film depicting the Jews as hordes of sewer-dwelling rats. He filmed Hitler's election campaign of 1932, the first in European history to be conducted by airplane, and gave it its slogan, *Hitler Over Germany*.

Perhaps the greatest stroke of Nazi propaganda was Leni Riefenstahl's film of the 1934 party congress at Nuremberg, entitled *Triumph des Willens* (*The Triumph of the Will*). In the early years of the war Goebbels also used film to motivate audiences with pictures of German tanks sweeping everything before them.

However, not every propaganda trick was successful for the Nazis. The Berlin Olympics of 1936 were supposed to show the physical superiority of the Aryan race over all others. Unfortunately for the Nazis, the star of the Olympics was the African-American track athlete Jesse Owens, who won five gold medals.

For example, after the fall of Mussolini in September 1943, roughly 600,000 Italian soldiers in Nazi-occupied Crete and in Greece and other parts of the Balkans were given the choice of fighting alongside the Germans or working as slave labor for the Reich. Most of them willingly surrendered their arms. Under Speer's direction the production of armaments tripled. Still, the economy as a whole never realized its full potential.

The War and German Morale

On September 1, 1939, there was no rejoicing on the streets of Berlin when news broke that German troops had invaded Poland. The German people had applauded Hitler for getting what he had wanted in the Rhineland, in Austria, and in Czechoslovakia without going to war. The success of the early Blitzkrieg campaigns of 1939 and 1940 helped them to believe that peace would come quickly, however. For a while the flow of materials and forced labor from the occupied countries in both the east and west helped to fend off hardship at home. The mood shifted, however, during and after the invasion of the Soviet Union in 1941.

In 1942, as the first Allied bombs fell on German cities, people realized that Germany would struggle to find the resources to win the war. Yet at the Berlin Sports Palace in October, Hitler told the German people that the back of the Soviet Union had been broken and that Russia would never rise again. When Germans were asked to donate winter clothing for the troops in December, 1942, they were shocked. Had the Führer failed to provide for his soldiers?

Alarming rumors of experiments performed on old and mentally ill people in hospitals began to spread. The Allied bombing of German cities after 1942, the defeat at Stalingrad in 1943, dire shortages in food and manpower, combined with other worries, sapped morale. Even so, years of indoctrination allowed the Nazi faithful to keep their trust in Hitler right to the end.

KEY FIGURES

ALBERT SPEER (1905–1981)

Albert Speer was the official Nazi architect. He was Hitler's protégé, close friend, and trusted political ally. Speer was never a Nazi ideologue. Instead, he was attracted by Hitler's dream of redesigning Berlin as the capital of a great German empire. "I was wild to accomplish things at twenty-eight-years-old (in 1933). I would have sold my soul, like Faust."

Speer's most famous design was the magnificently colonnaded Nuremberg Stadium, where Goebbels staged his propaganda rallies.

Speer was the only leading Nazi on trial at Nuremberg after the war to admit responsibility for the Nazi regime's actions. He spent twenty years in Spandau prison in West Berlin. He died in 1981 in London.

German Resistance to Hitler

Resistance in the face of Nazi terror, especially during the war years, is difficult to measure. Passive resistance may include nonconformity, emigration, or suicide. Active resistance includes individual bravery. Georg Elser tried to assassinate Hitler in 1939 by placing a bomb in the Munich Beer Hall, where Hitler annually celebrated the 1923 putsch. Hitler escaped only because he left earlier than planned. The Munich university students of the "White Rose" group, led by Hans and Sophie Scholl, distributed anti-Nazi leaflets. Discovered in 1943, they were executed for treason.

Organized resistance to the Nazi regime in Germany was formed by three groups: the Communists; right-wing, aristocratic groups; and the military. Alone among the political parties, the Communists met in underground cells and developed propaganda against the regime. Associated with the Communists was a resistance and spy group called the "Red Orchestra." They were exposed in 1942, and many of its members were executed. In total it is thought that about 20,000 Communists paid for resistance work with their lives.

Hitler escaped only because he left earlier than planned.

More powerful, and closer to the centers of Nazi operations, were the conservative nationalists. They were upholders of Prussian tradition and hated the destruction of the old German way of life. Their objectives are hard to identify because little was written down. But one group in particular, the Kreisau Circle of notables led by Count Helmuth James von Moltke, did have a clear manifesto: the military defeat of Germany as the prelude to the rebuilding of Europe.

The German military was best placed for effective resistance. A number of senior officers, along with diplomats and civil servants, tried to stage a coup against Hitler in 1938. It failed partly because those involved could not persuade the British government to back them. The Munich agreement, which allowed Hitler to bask in popularity, put an end to any immediate hopes of overthrowing him.

Another failed attempt by army officers to stage a coup occured in November 1939. But resistance to the regime became more and more difficult as the war went on and the state intensified its crackdown on dissidents. In July 1944 another bomb plot to assassinate Adolf Hitler failed. Soon after, about 5,000 former ministers, deputies, mayors, and Nazi officials were rounded up and put in prison.

Resistance to Hitler took many forms. This 1939 poster from the Federal Theatre Project advertises the play, "Day Is Darkness" by George Fess. The bottom script is in Yiddish.

THE KREISAU CIRCLE

The Kreisau Circle was an informal think tank of about twenty-five to thirty Germans united by a hatred of Nazism. They wanted to replace Nazism with a more enlightened system of government. The group took its name from Kreisau (now Krzyzowa, Poland), the estate of Count Helmuth James von Moltke, where its meetings took place.

Von Moltke, born in 1907 to an English mother, was a great-nephew of Helmuth Karl von Moltke, a great Prussian military planner. A liberal thinker, he rejected National Socialism and expected its power to wane. In 1940, when the Blitzkrieg convinced him otherwise, he linked up with others like him to form the Kreisau Circle.

The Circle recruited from conservative friends and local landowners, from officials who had strong links with pockets of resistance, from trade unions, from the law and teaching professions, from the clergy, and from the government. The Circle hoped that a core group representing a wide cross section of society might provide a way to rebuild a post-Hitler Germany.

During 1942 and 1943 the Kreisau Circle drew up a constitution of sorts called *The Fundamental Principles of the New Order.* It described how a new Germany might be governed. At heart, its principles were Christian. (The Circle had links with Dietrich Bonhoffer. Bonhoffer was a German minister who vehemently opposed Hitler and Nazism. He was executed in 1943.) Out of fidelity to Christian doctrine, the Circle at first shrank from any plot to kill Hitler. Later, as Nazi horrors spread, and Germany's military defeat loomed, certain members supported the bomb plot of July 20, 1944. Almost all in the Circle were arrested and executed: some for their part in the bomb plot, and others, like Moltke, for planning a future after Nazism.

Mussolini's Ambitions

Mussolini imagined that a German victory would bring Italy the gains he dreamed of. More importantly, Mussolini felt that the survival of Italian Fascism might depend on a Nazi victory. Yet he also hesitated. He worried that Italy might eventually have to fight Germany to avoid becoming a state of the Nazis. In early 1940, he claimed he was waiting like a cat, watching its prey and choosing when to pounce.

Hitler fascinated Mussolini. Hitler, though, knew how to appeal to Mussolini's vanity. In March 1940, when Mussolini urged Hitler to make war in the east and draw back from the western front, Hitler waited two months to reply. Mussolini chose a good moment to join Hitler because France was just two weeks from surrender. Mussolini wanted to be in on the victory at little cost to Italy.

Mussolini saw himself as a great military leader, and for that reason blundered into Greece in 1940 without informing Hitler. Out of pride, he refused to accept any German military support in the Mediterranean. Disaster after disaster followed, including the loss of Ethiopia. What little popular support there was for war drained away.

A major flaw in Mussolini's conduct of the war was that he tried to do everything himself. By 1943 he was not only the generalissimo, but also the head of six major departments of government. Trying to manage everything, he was able to manage very little.

EYEWITNESS

IGOR MARKEVITCH

The Italian conductor Igor Markevitch began a memoir of Italy under Fascism in 1946. His lack of respect for Mussolini shows through his sarcasm in his description of Mussolini making a speech to justify the war with Greece.

He mounts the rostrum. The Duce speakes! Duce! Duce! Duce! The shouts in the Chamber begin anew. He gives the sign for silence. The Chamber curbs its joy. All Italy relapses into silence.

Everything has come to a standstill throughout the Kingdom. The factories are motionless. The peasants are waiting in the village market-places; the astonished oxen have leisure to chase their flies. . .

The voice begins: "Italians on land, on sea, on air, in all parts of the globe, listen! The war with Greece was necessary. . . A single word must be engraved in your hearts: Victory!"

People sigh and continue on their way. Italy can begin moving again. The factories resume work, . . and the oxen amble off to the fields. Everyone is a little gloomier than usual. why are we alive, anyway?

SALÒ: MUSSOLINI'S LAST "EMPIRE"

After his fall from power in July 1943, Mussolini was held at a number of places by the new government. In September he was freed by a Nazi rescue party. He was taken to Hitler's bunker in East Prussia, where he announced his resumption of power. He called upon Italy to eliminate the traitors who had driven him from office. He wanted to return to Rome, but the Germans sent him to the small town of Gargano, on Lake Garda instead. There he "ruled" as a Nazi puppet over the "Italian Social Republic." In fact, he was isolated even from Nazi-occupied north Italy, which was based a few miles away at Salò.

Mussolini had no control over the affairs of the Salò Republic, a police state run with Italian collaborators by the Nazi proconsul, Rudolf Rahn, and the army commander, General Wolff. The Germans tolerated him only because keeping Fascism alive in Italy was helpful. They annexed Trieste and Alto Adige. Those were the Italian lands that Mussolini had thought an alliance with Germany would help him keep. Mussolini continued to work long hours and to live, as he always had, without luxuries. He was unrepentant. He remained hopeful that Italian people would return to Fascism as the best way to fight Communism.

Mussolini was captured at Dongo, on Lake Como near the Italian–Swiss border, by Communist partisans and executed on April 28, 1945. Ironically, the American liberators of Nazi-occupied Italy were just a few hours away.

At his fall Mussolini blamed the Italian people for being unwarlike. But he had provided no strategic or economic basis for war. He placed his faith in the Nazis, instead of in the Italian people. "People endured the horrors of war as a fatality, a volcanic eruption, a calamity falling on them from another planet," the Italian conductor Igor Markevitch wrote in 1946. Mussolini's name came to be scarcely mentioned. By the end, "People discussed his war as though it were being fought in Peru. Already forgotten by a people he had betrayed, he was now drifting aimlessly, a derelict piece of wreckage, while Fascism was beating its last roll on a cracked bass drum."

The Italian Economy in Ruins

Mussolini took Italy into the war in June 1940. The announcement was made with so little warning that many ships in the Italian merchant marine did not have time to return to safe harbors. A third of Italy's merchant shipping was lost before any troops saw action. It was not a good omen. But what mattered more was that the Italian economy was not geared up for a long war. Mussolini, like Hitler, imagined that the war would be over quickly. So the Italian army became involved in long, costly campaigns in the Balkans and Africa.

After his fall from power when the war was nearly over, Mussolini admitted that he had asked Italy to fight with outdated weapons. And he confessed that even the new Carro Armato tank introduced during the war was a failure. For all his belief in war as the making of men and nations, Mussolini had done little to prepare Italy for it.

In a country that lacked raw materials and was far less industrialized than Britain and even France, it was hard to believe that a ministry for war production was not established until 1943. By then it was too late to have much effect. Since the economy was not on a war footing, demand for munitions constantly outstripped supply. By 1943 Italy had only four hundred fighter planes in service because the aircraft industry was unable to keep up with losses. By then, too, the merchant marine had nearly vanished.

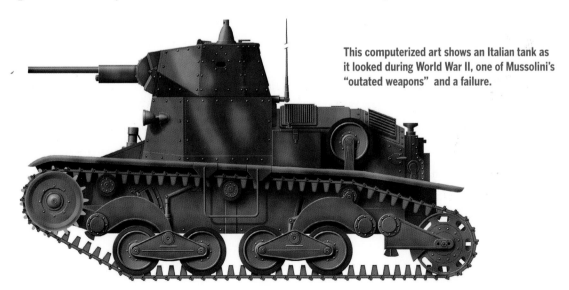

This computerized art shows an Italian tank as it looked during World War II, one of Mussolini's "outated weapons" and a failure.

Although Mussolini intended to disrupt daily life as little as possible, from the beginning, food and clothing shortages combined with inflation to empty Italian pockets. The average Italian income in 1942 was about $400 a year. A pair of shoes cost $35, nearly a tenth of the annual income. In December of that year workers and farmers went on strike for higher wages. Their slogan was "For bread, peace, and freedom."

Riots caused by food shortages extended throughout the land. In the countryside peasants complained about the forced collection of grains and other crops. Amid the shortages, workers were outraged to find that luxury goods for the rich were still being sold. As late as 1943, some units of the army were without boots and recruits could not be called up because there was no footwear for them. But leather shoes were still available in the shops. Rationing was introduced, but it was much too late.

Riots caused by food shortages extended throughout the land.

Two events held a grim warning for Mussolini. In the spring of 1942 a number of bankers and industrialists deserted Mussolini and the Fascists. They made up the Party of Action, which worked for the formation of a republic with a new constitution. A year later, a general strike was called in the industrial cities of Milan and Turin. Strong public support for the workers powerfully indicated that Mussolini's days as Il Duce were numbered.

Military Rule in Japan

When World War II began in Europe, the Japanese prime minister, Prince Konoye, was one of just a few politicians who had a desire to stand up to the army. Konoye was eager to keep Japan out of war, but the military was too strong for him. He felt let down by Emperor Hirohito. Out of step with Japan's aggressiveness, Konoye gave way to Hideki Tojo.

When Tojo became prime minister in October 1941, Japan became a military dictatorship in all but name. The government remained what it had been for some years: a mix of the armed forces, big business interests, and bureaucrats.

HIDEKI TOJO

Hideki Tojo, who became Japan's wartime prime minister, was one of the men most responsible for the destruction of democracy in Japan and the resulting rule by the army.

Born in 1884, Hideki Tojo was the son of a samurai. His father had served the Meiji emperor in the late nineteenth century. Tojo was notorious for his scruffy looks, thinking nothing of being seen in public in a wrinkled uniform with baggy trousers and in unpolished boots. But he was an inspiring public speaker, an able administrator, and a respected military field commander.

Nicknamed Kamisori (the Razor), Tojo gained fame as a disciplinarian in his position as chief of police in the Kwantung army in Manchuria, and later from 1938 to 1940 as chief of staff in Manchuria. As head of the *Tosei-ha* (Control Faction) in the military he supported an expansionist policy in China and Southeast Asia. He also agreed that Japan had to prepare for war against Great Britain and the United States. Tojo apparently had a sincere vision of a Greater East Asia as a free association of independent states.

Tojo became war minister in 1940, urging closer collaboration with Germany and Italy. With reluctant help from Vichy France, Japan occupied bases in Indochina in July 1941. increasing tensions with the United States.

During the summer and autumn of 1941 Tojo led the war party that brought down the government of Prince Konoye. His challenge to Konoye's belief that the Japanese naval commanders did not want war led to the political crisis that brought him to the prime ministership in October, 1941. "It is just as they say," Emperor Hirohito remarked on appointing him, "You can't control a tiger unless you enter its lair."

Tojo was responsible, along with Hirohito, for Japan's going to war, though the attack on Pearl Harbor was kept a secret from the emperor. At first his leadership helped ensure Japanese victories in the Pacific. Later American successes in the region, especially in the Mariana Islands, led to his downfall in July 1944. He made a bungled suicide attempt after Japan's surrender. After being tried as a war criminal, he and six others were executed.

In particular, the *zaibatsu* (the small group of large corporations whom the government allowed to control industry) remained strong. There is little evidence, however, that business leaders sought to reign in the power of the army. The zaibatsu understood that its aims—to find foreign sources of raw materials and overseas markets for Japanese goods—could be achieved only by military conquest. One of the reasons for going to war in the Pacific was to obtain control of raw materials, like oil and rubber, from Asian colonies of the Western powers. The army and big business worked together well. The emperor, the politicians, and the bureaucracy all declined in influence. By the end of the war there were only two politicians on the Supreme War Council that governed the whole of Japan: the prime minister and the foreign minister.

At the end of the war the workforce was mostly made up of women, children, Koreans, and prisoners of war.

Japan had been on a war footing for the past decade. In July 1940 the manufacture of luxury goods was banned; the sale of luxuries was stopped in October. Driving for pleasure was also ended in the summer of 1940, and six months before Pearl Harbor private cars were banned from the streets. Rubber could not be used for shoes. Metal plumbing and other fixtures were stripped from homes. The government even took away small items such as safety pins and eyeglass rims.

In the end, the Japanese people put in long hours in the factories, and the shipyards and munitions plants delivered two hundred Japanese submarines and other warships and 70,000 aircraft. However, Japan was unable to match the industrial output of the Allied powers. Too many skilled workers were drafted into the army. Of the remaining workers, nearly half worked in agriculture. At the end of the war the workforce was mostly made up of women, children, Koreans, and prisoners of war.

Japan in Defeat

Emperor Hirohito made a historic radio broadcast on August 11, 1945. He announced that Japan had accepted the Allies' demand of an unconditional surrender. This announcement might have been expected to provoke a national reaction of dismay. Only two days before the emperor had listened to the army chiefs, one after another, plead against surrender. Yet, Japan was surrounded on all sides, attacked by the Soviet Union and losing Manchuria, and the United States had dropped atomic bombs on Hiroshima and Nagasaki by the United States. The war minister, General Anami, even held out the possibility of victory. The country, Anami urged, would not surrender. "Our army will not submit to demobilization. Our men will not lay down their arms. And since they know they are not permitted to surrender, since they know that a fighting man who surrenders is liable to extremely heavy punishment, there is really no alternative for us but to continue the war."

Anami was wrong. Civilians were tired of living on rations, without new clothing, without gasoline for their cars, with little more than rice and a few vegetables to eat. By 1945 there were many districts where even rice was no longer available. People ate pumpkins instead. Overseas, hundreds of thousands of Japanese soldiers laid down their arms.

The Japanese suffered defeat with remarkable stoicism, and they accepted Allied occupation. A small number of Japanese airmen dropped leaflets on Tokyo calling for resistance and not surrender. The U.S. Army's peaceful entry into Tokyo was, however, the beginning of an astonishingly harmonious occupation of one major power by another. In their quiet acceptance of the enemy in their midst the Japanese people displayed an understanding of necessity.

The Japanese suffered defeat with remarkable stoicism, and they accepted Allied occupation.

Japan was devastated by the war. Almost 2 million soldiers and civilians had been killed and many of Japan's major cities lay in ruins, with 5 million homes destroyed. Food was scarce and the population faced starvation. It was againstw this background that General Douglas MacArthur of the United States Army was installed as the commander of the occupying forces. He successfully brought back 3 million Japanese soldiers from abroad, relieved food shortages, and set the foundations for a demilitarized, democratic postwar Japan.

▶Nightly Axis air raids damaged British industry, but the attacks served only to steel civilian resolve against Hitler. Similar courage was exhibited in abundance in the USSR, in the face of appalling human suffering.

6

Allied Home Fronts in Europe, 1939 to 1945

KEY PEOPLE	KEY PLACES
Winston Churchill	London. England
Lord Beaverbrook	Leningrad (St. Petersburg), USSR (Russia)
Joseph Stalin	

World War II has been called "the People's War." Never before had warfare affected the lives of civilians so directly. In Britain more civilians than military personnel died in the twelve months after the start of the Blitz. People's lives were controlled by the state as never before. In the USSR the ordinary freedoms of daily life had long since been restricted, but Soviet heroism on the home front matched that displayed by any other country.

Emergency Powers in Britain

In May 1939 military conscription, or the peacetime draft, was introduced within Britain for the first time. In May 1940 an Emergency Powers Act gave the government almost unlimited authority to control the lives of citizens and property. War produced in Britain a kind of democratic authoritarianism. Civil liberties were given up for the common good.

At the outbreak of war, months before passing the Emergency Powers Act, the British government ordered the evacuation from cities of anyone who did not need to stay. All schoolchildren, pregnant women, and mothers with children under the age of five were sent to the countryside. There, they were placed in private homes. Householders had no choice, although they were paid to house and feed the evacuees. In the first three days of evacuation, in September 1939, roughly 1.5 million evacuees, many of them children, were sent from London by train.

In September 1940, at the start of the Blitz, a second wave of evacuations took place.

More than 3,000 children were evacuated to Australia, Canada, and South Africa under a government-run program, the Children's Overseas Reception Board (CORB). Churchill opposed CORB, regarding it as "defeatist." His opinion was validated after the night of September 17, 1940, when the *City of Benares*, carrying ninety children from Liverpool to Canada, was sunk by a U-boat. Just thirteen of the children survived. After that, overseas evacuations were discontinued.

In September 1940, at the start of the Blitz, a second wave of evacuations took place. This time it was largely voluntary and unplanned. In the country as a whole, another 1 million people fled from the bombing. There were no more mass evacuations until 1944.

For some time the British government had been working on plans to protect civilians from air raids. The money spent by the government on what became known as ARP (air-raid precautions) rose from $38 million in 1937–1938 to $204 million in 1939–1940. Most ARP activities, such as rescue parties and first-aid sections, were at first carried out by volunteers. From January 1941 on, however, every commercial company was required to provide a list of its employees who would stand watch for fires from incendiary bombs. Six months before that, the government "froze" all the voluntary ARP services. Once in, a volunteer was no longer allowed to leave. Meanwhile, more and more men and women were drafted into the services.

> *Six months before that, the government "froze" all the voluntary ARP services. Once in, a volunteer was no longer allowed to leave.*

FRANCES FAVIELL

Early on in the Blitz, on September 14, 1940, a large church in the Chelsea district of London was hit by a German bomber. After the war Frances Faviell, a volunteer in an ARP [air-raid precautions] unit recalled the horrific scenes and the dedication of volunteers there.

The bomb was recorded by one of us telephonists in the Control Center at 6:35 P.M. The message said that there was fire and casualties trapped in Holy Redeemer Church in Upper Cheyne Row. Requests followed in rapid succession for ambulances, blankets to cover the dead, fire services, and reports came in that there were many casualties...

The work of the ARP Services that night was magnificent—by nine o'clock in the evening the casualties were all extricated and laid in the grounds of the church with the Home Guard in charge...

After a heavy raid with many casualties, such as this one, there was a task for which we were sometimes detailed... and to which both our Commandants disliked having to send us. This was to help piece the bodies together in preparation for burial. The bodies—or rather the pieces—were in temporary mortuaries. It was a grim task. Betty Compton felt that we were too young and inexperienced for such a terrible undertaking—but someone had to do it and we were sent in pairs when it became absolutely necessary. Betty asked me if I would go as I had studied anatomy at the Slade [an art college]. The first time I went my partner was a girl I did not know very well called Sheila. It was grim, although it was all made as businesslike and rapid as possible. We had somehow to form a body for burial so that the relatives (without seeing it) could imagine that their loved one was more or less intact for the purpose. But it was a very difficult task—there were so many pieces missing and, as one of the mortuary attendants said, "Proper jigsaw puzzle, ain't it, miss?" The stench was the worst thing about it—that, and having to realize that these frightful pieces of flesh had once been living, breathing people...

Transcript from the documentary film *A Chelsea Concerto* (1959).

Britain under Fire

The German Blitz of Britain—the country's worst foreign attack since 1667— lasted from early September 1940 to the middle of May 1941. London, the capital city, was bombed every night from September 7 to November 2, 1940. Then German planes switched to bombing the industrial cities of the north and then the western ports. The last heavy raid of the Blitz hit Birmingham on May 16, 1941. After that date, the raids themselves were often less trouble than what people had to do to prepare for them.

Parts of East London, and other cities, like Coventry, were devasted.

The German bombing of Britain was not nearly as powerful and effective as the bombing of Germany later in the war. The German bomb still caused much destruction, the worst of it from incendiary bombs. More than 3.5 million houses were damaged. Even landmarks like Buckingham Palace, home of the king and queen, and the House of Commons, seat of the British parliament, were hit. Parts of East London, and other cities, like Coventry, were devastated. One night's air raid left only seven houses in the whole of the Scottish shipbuilding town of Clydebank undamaged. In the first four months of the Blitz, more than 13,000 civilians lost their lives in London. By its end the national toll was over 30,000. Civilians were caught up in the fighting in World War II as never before. When the war ended in 1945, 60,000 civilians and 35,000 merchant seamen had died, while military casualties, at 300,000, were fewer than half the total in World War I. People with yards were able to take refuge from the Luftwaffe in an Anderson shelter—a partially buried, corrugated iron tunnel. Those living in urban housing had to wait for the Morrison shelter, a small steel cage for indoor use that was not available until the spring of 1941. When Londoners ignored the ban on sleeping in subway stations overnight and refused to leave, the authorities turned them into dormitories. Camp beds, toilets, and food were provided. Some city dwellers fled to the countryside when dusk fell, returning to their homes in the morning.

People whose homes had been destroyed took refuge in "Rest Centers" in schools and church halls. Other hardships included getting through the

These children, accompanied by an adult, look skyward for German planes. They are taking refuge in an English bomb shelter during the Blitz, 1940.

winter in unheated buildings and working in ill-lit, poorly ventilated basement rooms. Although the general health of the population improved during the war due to a healthier diet, tuberculosis increased sharply.

The Blitz affected daily life in many ways. There were the gas masks issued to everyone, the constant wailing of air-raid sirens, and the nightly "blackout." On the assumption, probably mistaken, that every bit of light would help German pilots find their bombing targets, no home was allowed to show any light. The blackout's purpose was to lift morale. It made everyone feel that there was a part for him or her to play in the war effort. When the Blitz was over, the British people remained united in their determination to resist Nazism.

The British Economy at War

In 1938 Britain's air force and navy were well equipped, though the army needed attention. It took time for factories to be rebuilt into plants capable of making tanks and artillery and for labor to be diverted to them. But within a few months of the outbreak of war the government had the powers needed to place the economy on a war footing. Rationing, conscription of labor, and controls over imports and exports were all under government control.

Winston Churchill created only one new ministry when he became prime minister in May 1940. The Ministry of Air Production was created to act for the RAF as the Ministry of Supply did for the British army. Under the leadership of Lord Beaverbrook, the ministry worked wonders. By 1941 British arms production greatly surpassed Germany's, especially in tanks and airplanes. On joining the war cabinet in August 1940, Beaverbrook insisted that factories be moved from industrial areas and scattered throughout the country. By 1943, when war production had risen nearly tenfold since September 1939, more British manufacturing was devoted to war than ever before.

The Ministry of Food, under Lord Woolton, rationed food so that everyone should receive equal supplies.

Under the pressure of war Britain operated an economic system that was as socialist as anything in the Soviet Union. The small staff of the Board of Trade, for example, which was used to presiding over a relatively free market, suddenly had to regulate all retail trade. It set standards for the manufacture of inexpensive, uniform furniture, and it controlled the distribution of clothing, which was in very short supply. To make agricultural production more efficient, 4 million acres (1.62 million hectares) of land were converted from livestock to vegetable farming. The Ministry of Food, under Lord Woolton, rationed food so that everyone should receive equal supplies. The number of school meals doubled in 1940–1941. Woolton's department also improved the national diet. Everyone received daily milk, orange juice, and cod-liver oil. They were encouraged to bake the "Woolton pie," made from potatoes, parsnips, and herbs.

Two outstanding achievements of "war socialism" were the allocation of labor and the conscription of women into the work force. These were the contribution of the labor minister, Ernest Bevin. Also, the government responded to coal shortages in 1942 and 1943 by controlling supplies to consumers and giving miners a raise in pay. Young men removed from conscription lists and sent down the coal mines became known as "Bevin boys." Despite a new purchase tax on consumer goods and a rise in income tax, most workers were better off during the war than they had been during the Depression. Unemployment virtually disappeared.

> *... most workers were better off than they had been during the Depression. Unemployment virtually disappeared.*

The government, though concerned about inflation, wisely allowed earnings to rise while prices held steady. Personal consumer spending declined by 15 percent during 1939–1941. The decline was

LORD BEAVERBROOK

KEY FIGURES

Lord Beaverbrook (1879–1964) was a wealthy, Canadian-born investment banker who owned the British *Daily Express* newspaper. In 1940 he was appointed to Winston Churchill's war cabinet as the minister of aircraft production.

At the Air Ministry Beaverbrook made an impression as a man who got things done. He switched the slow production of bombers to the much quicker production of fighter planes. In aircraft factories, laborers had to work ten hours a day, seven days a week. Because he had Churchill's backing, Lord Beaverbrook was able to claim priority for his ministry over other departments. This manner of government worked well for a time.

It also contributed to victory in the Battle of Britain in 1940.

Beaverbrook was a bully to some, but his enthusiasm and self-confidence rubbed off on people. He remained in the war cabinet as minister of supply, then minister of war production, until February 1942. Beaverbrook had no political following. His high office in the government depended entirely on the favor of the prime minister. He lost that favor when he attempted to take control of the Labor Ministry from Ernest Bevin. Bevin was the workers' champion, and Churchill was bound to back him. Beaverbrook resigned. While he and Bevin were never friends, they were the two ministers who helped Churchill the most in putting Britain on the road to victory.

in part because fewer goods were available to buy, but also because of a patriotic desire to respond to the government's appeal for saving. Consumers spent less on food, clothing, household goods, and driving, but more on things such as the movies, where they could watch the latest newsreels.

Morale on the British Home Front

The chief purpose of Hitler's air raids on British cities was to break the spirit of the people and bring the British government to a settlement. If anything, the heavy bombing, night after night, mostly stiffened the public's resolve. Men and women of all classes worked side by side as volunteers to defeat the enemy. At the height of the Blitz, a few British voices did speak in favor of a peace settlement with Germany. A motion in parliament to sue for peace in December 1940, was defeated by 341 votes to 4.

KEY FIGURES

WILLIAM JOYCE (LORD HAW-HAW)

Great efforts were made to give the British people entertainment during the war years. But nothing provided as much interest as some of the propaganda broadcasts from Germany. They were made by the pro-Nazi Irish American William Joyce. He was nicknamed "Lord Haw-Haw" by a British journalist because of his aristocratic nasal drawl.

Joyce was born in the United States of Irish parents. The family moved back to Ireland when he was three and then settled in southeast London. In the early 1920s, Joyce joined a tiny group called the British Fascisti. In the 1930s he was the right-hand man of Oswald Mosley, the leader of the British Union of Fascists. When war broke out he went to Berlin to fight against the Jews and Communism.

Within two weeks Joyce was broadcasting regularly across the English Channel. "Jairmany calling" he would begin, in his fake aristocratic accent, going on to denounce Churchill, vilify the "Jeeoos," (Jews) and proclaim the inevitable victory of the Nazis. For his work he received the very generous salary of $250 a month, and several items of luxury. Almost to the end "Haw-Haw" continued to predict an Axis victory, but in 1945 he was arrested and charged with high treason. Had he not falsely declared himself to have been Irish-born, he would, as an American, have been beyond the reach of British justice. He was convicted and executed at Wandsworth prison, London.

By the end of May 1941, people were cheered by the belief that Britain had seen the last of Hitler. Having survived the Blitz, the country felt it could endure anything. The high morale in Britain owed much to Winston Churchill. His speeches promising "blood, toil, tears, and sweat," delivered to the House of Commons and broadcast by radio, helped Britain through his country's "finest hour." His tone of voice was reassuring as were the upbeat cadences of his sentences. Throughout the remainder of the war his appearances in newsreels also cheered the British people. In the newsreels, Churchill was mixing with his soldiers at the front, whether on the Normandy beaches or in the deserts of North Africa. To encourage and reward heroism on the home front, the government introduced a new medal, the George Cross (named for the reigning monarch, George VI), for acts of civilian bravery. Veterans of World War I flocked to join the Home Guard, which had a total of 1 million volunteers by the summer of 1940.

Government advertising urged the British people to "Dig For Victory." This slogan encouraged Britons to grow their own vegetables and to fight inflation by buying National Savings bonds rather than spend their money. Not all the propaganda made sense, especially the posters that asked people to keep their mouths shut, with slogans like "Careless Talk Costs Lives." Helping to boost morale, however, in a country divided by class, was the sense that everyone could pull together for victory. Rationing of food and clothing, although it was introduced only because of

This poster from 1942 shows how everyone in Britain was called on to make sacrifices for the war effort. Women and children could also help "Produce for Victory!"

"This is everybody's war. The enemy has made it so. May you never know what it means to be a refugee . . . to be hungry . . . to be homeless. Be sure this never happens to you!"

PRODUCE FOR VICTORY!

shortages, was a kind of social welfare provision. The lines outside food stores became a symbol of national unity.

Though workers fared well in the war—their pay rose, while housing rents were frozen in 1939—the wealthier fared less well. They did not enjoy private driving or foreign travel, they had few domestic servants, and their clothing was less fine. They were taxed heavily with a new purchase tax for luxuries. However, if the British wealthy grumbled, they did so in private. Perhaps never in British history did the nation appear so united as it did from 1940 to 1945.

The Economy of the USSR

World War II left the Soviet Union in ruins. Twenty million people died, and half the cities, railroads, mines, and factories were destroyed. Huge swaths of farmland were left devastated. Part of that was the work of the Soviet government itself. The first six months of the war were a disaster as German tanks rolled into Soviet territory along a broad front. The Soviet government had been ill prepared for war on such a scale. Ironically, under the terms of the Soviet–Nazi pact, the Soviet Union had sent oil, iron, and timber to Germany from 1939 to 1941. Stalin accumulated some war stocks

During World War II, the Soviet Union experienced changes in agricultural production. In 1942 Germany's territorial gains within the USSR caused production to fall to 40 percent of previous levels.

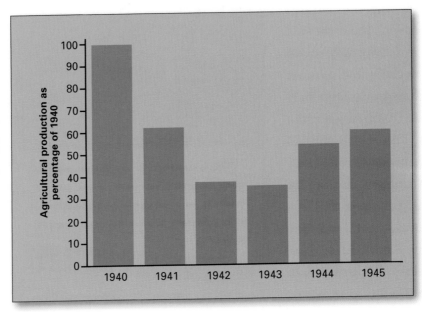

and expanded Soviet armaments between 1939 and 1941. But, he could not match German war production during the same period.

To make the best of things, retreating Soviet forces destroyed much heavy industry, like mining and metallurgy. Stalin, in his radio broadcast on July 3, 1941, made a reference to the defense of Moscow against Napoleon in 1812. He asked the people to "scorch the earth." He added, "All rolling stock must be evacuated. The enemy must not be left a single engine, a single railway car, a single pound of grain, or gallon of fuel." Guerrilla sabotage groups were formed, but the strategy was not entirely successful. Nearly half of the country's industrial and agricultural production was in enemy control by October 1941. Then, in the last months of the war in 1945, industrial plants were blown up for a second time—this time by the Germans in the face of advancing Red Army troops. The Germans also burned down entire villages.

The Germans also burned down entire villages.

From the terrible beginning to the war, however, the Soviet economy made a strong recovery. In 1942 tank production doubled and air production tripled. By 1945 the Soviets had surpassed Germany in the manufacture of tanks and aircraft. The Soviet people were used to five-year economic plans with their emphasis on heavy industry, as well as having economic decisions made by the central government. The chief of secret police, Lavrenti Beria, supervised the war economy. People were told what jobs they had to do. Once they had taken jobs, they were not allowed to leave them.

For ordinary people, one of the worst parts of the war was the disruption of family life, caused when the factories were removed to the east, beyond the Ural mountains, out of the Germans' reach. More than 6 million workers were uprooted when 1,500 factories were transplanted in this way. But the rapid industrialization of the eastern provinces enabled Soviet arms production to increase by 600 percent between 1942 and 1945.

The Soviet economy relied on Allied aid. At first both the shortage of supplies, especially in Britain, and the difficulty of getting them transported restricted what the Soviet Union received. British ships had to make a dangerous passage through the Arctic Ocean to the ports of Archangel and Murmansk. In order to move supplies via a southern ocean route through Iran, British and Soviet troops occupied Iran in August 1941. The Trans-Iranian railroad, linking the Persian Gulf to the Caspian Sea, became the most important supply line, delivering to the southern part of the Soviet Union. By the end of the war, through various routes, the United States had sent about $11 billion worth of lend-lease aid to the USSR.

Stalin and Soviet Morale

Ever since the Bolshevik revolution of 1917, the USSR had avoided references to the old czarist days. Everything good in Soviet society had its origins in November 1917. In the crisis of war, however, Stalin decided to raise the morale of the Russian people by evoking memories of the defeat of Napoleon in 1812 by the Russian Imperial Army. "Let the manly images of our great ancestors inspire you in this war," he said in a speech in Red Square on November 6, 1941, as the Germans began to assault the capital. The defense of the motherland, rather than the march of the Communist revolution, became the battle cry.

Throughout World War II, the United States provided food, supplies, and armament to the Allies, especially Britain and the Soviet Union.

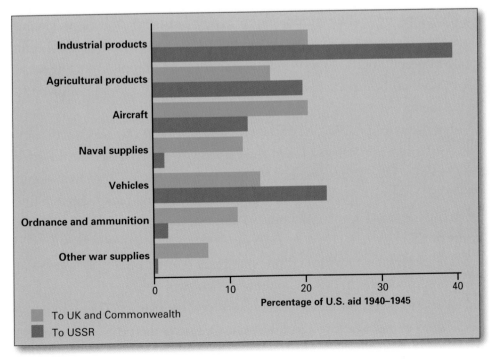

The Russian people responded with a kind of patriotism. Then morale suffered a shock in early November 1941, when the news spread that the government had evacuated Moscow. Riots in the streets followed, food stores were looted, and numerous Communists tore up their party membership cards. Morale was restored when it was learned that Stalin himself remained in the Kremlin. The Russian people took that as a sign that Stalin's will to victory was unshaken. His speeches to the Russian people had a similar effect that Churchill's had on the British people.

In terms of home defense, Russia had its own, better organized version of the British Home Guard. In 1941 when German troops reached the outskirts of Moscow, they were met by the *opolcheniye*, literally "people's militia." The militias were volunteers with rifles and tools who flowed out of the factories to defend the motherland. Despite some collaboration with the enemy in certain areas, the people's loyalty to the Stalinist regime was greater than expected.

That the USSR made it through the first critical year of the war owed something to the Russian winter, but more was owed to the spirit of the people and their leader. "It is very fortunate for Russia in her agony," Churchill said of Stalin, "to have this great rugged war chief at her head. He is a man of massive outstanding personality, suited to the somber and stormy time in which his life has been cast."

The People of Leningrad

Nowhere did the phrase "total war" come to be understood more deeply than in Leningrad, now known as St. Petersburg. Its people had to endure horrors on a scale unmatched in any other city in the Allied world. Hitler hated Leningrad, as it was the cradle of Bolshevism. He set out to destroy it by setting up an economic blockade around the city in September 1941.

During the siege, which lasted for nearly 900 days, 630,000 civilians died from cold and hunger and another 200,000 from German air raids. When food ran out, as it did the very first winter, workers were reduced to a ration of 9 ounces (225 g) of bread a day. Dogs and cats appeared on the menu, along with small birds and horsemeat. People were even accused of cannibalism.

For months and months the city was without electricity or fuel. The consequences of the siege were awful. Corpses were hauled to cemeteries on sleds. People fell dead in the streets and were left under the snow, producing epidemics of disease in the spring when the ice melted and the corpses began to rot. When spring came in April 1942, women picked anything edible that was growing, such as dandelions, nettles, and sorrel. Every available piece of land, in public and private, was used to grow vegetables. The city looked like a patchwork of farmland plots. However, the entire length of the city's broadest thoroughfare, the Nevsky Prospect, retained its elegant flowerbeds. People's spirits brightened, once the spring sun returned, when they were able once more to buy cut flowers.

The novelist Aleksandr Fadeyev wrote of the plight of the city's children.

The novelist Aleksandr Fadeyev wrote about the plight of the city's children. "The people of Leningrad, above all the women of Leningrad, can be proud that, in the conditions of the blockade, they saved the children. A considerable proportion of the child population had been evacuated from Leningrad—I am not referring to them. I refer rather to the small children of Leningrad who sustained all the burdens of their own city."

A network of kindergartens was set up to which the starving city gave what it had. Fadeyev visited many of them, but more often he watched children playing in the city's parks and squares. "In April [1942], when I first saw the Leningrad children, they had already emerged from the most difficult period of their lives, but the hard experience of the winter was still imprinted on their faces and was still reflected in the games. It was reflected in the way many of the children played all by themselves, in the way that, even in their collective games, they played in silence, with grave faces. . . those faces and eyes told one more than could be gathered from all the stories of the horrors of famine."

Pro-German Feeling in the USSR

The Russian people may have rallied to Stalin and the war against Germany. But other nationalities within the Soviet Union did not. There were places, especially in the south, where the invading Nazi divisions were hailed as liberators. Ukraine had been a stronghold of White (Menshevik) resistance to the "Red" Bolshevik revolution of 1917. Peasant families there had suffered from the forced collectivization of the farms and the famine of the early 1930s. Many Ukrainians thought that the Russian Communists had been guilty of something close to genocide.

The Ukrainian peasants had not read *Mein Kampf*. They did not know that Hitler had marked out their land as the center of his slave empire. The German soldiers who marched into Ukraine in the summer of 1941 were welcomed with food and drink. The Ukrainians soon learned, however, what the Nazis were really like. Heinrich Himmler's Einsatzgruppen came in behind the army. Many thousands of civilians—Jews, Communists, intellectuals, and others—were shipped to the concentration camps of the Reich. Hitler's racist obsession turned some people who might have collaborated with his army into anti-Nazi partisans.

Hitler looked forward to settling Germans in the Crimean Peninsula, whose Black Sea resorts were a vacation destination. He wanted to turn it into a German colony. Russians made up only half of the population. There was much collaboration with the Germans in the region, especially among the Muslim Tartars who had lived there since the Middle Ages. The Russians had rounded up the Tartars by the thousands and sent them to

Hitler looked forward to settling Germans in the Crimean Peninsula. . .

the labor camps as political prisoners. Because of what happened to them, the Germans were able to recruit 20,000 Tartars into battalions whose chief function was to hunt down Communist partisans in the mountains.

However, many other Tartars fought for the Soviet Union. Even so, when the Red Army returned in the spring of 1944, pro- and anti-Russian

Tartars were treated the same. Collaborators, if they were accused by two people, were rounded up and executed without trial, their corpses hung from trees. On May 18, 1944, every Crimean Tartar—including four men recently decorated for war service as Heroes of the Soviet Union—was sent to central Asia. Also accused and deported to Siberia were several hundred thousand Chechens and Ingush from the Caucasus. Thousands died on the journey. The survivors were doomed to a lifetime of exile.

Women and the Allied War Effort

Women played a vital war role in Britain and in the Soviet Union. In 1941 British women between the ages of twenty and thirty were subject to call-up to the armed forces (or the police or fire services). Older women had to register for factory work. In 1943 the age for military service was changed to cover anyone between the ages of eighteen and fifty. By 1944 there were half a million women in the Women's Royal Navy Service, the Auxiliary Territorial Service, and the Women's Auxiliary Air Force. Another 200,000 women "dug for victory" in the Women's Land Army, and 260,000 worked in arms factories. It was almost impossible for a woman to avoid work. People imagined that it would take three women to do two men's work. In fact, women performed just as well as men, and their wartime experience had long-lasting effect.

People imagined that it would take three women to do two men's work. In fact, women performed just as well as men, and their wartime experience had long-lasting effect.

In the USSR 20 million men went to the front. They were replaced as workers on the home front by women—many of them schoolgirls—who made up more than half the labor force by 1945. This number of women in the work force was double the number in 1940. In February 1942, Soviet women between the ages of sixteen and forty-five were eligible for the draft. About 800,000 served in the military and another 200,000 as partisans in Nazi-occupied territory.

In the Red Army, women were treated as equals of men. They served on the front lines in all the major battles on Russian soil. This Russian woman sniper stands ready to take action against the enemy.

Soviet women served in combat alongside men, as snipers, tank drivers, and pilots. Some countries used women as test pilots. However, only the USSR sent women into combat. Two Soviet women's regiments became especially famous. The 586th Fighter Aviation Regiment, which included Lily Litviak, the "White Rose of Stalingrad," won high praise for its heroism in defense of the city. The 46th Guards Night Bomber Aviation Regiment, known in Germany as the "Night Witches," had to use outdated biplanes. Nevertheless, they were honored by the Soviet military for outstanding service.

▶ The USS *West Virginia* is in flames after the attack on Pearl Harbor, December 7, 1941. As the U.S. flag flies against the smoke-blackened sky, sailors ignore the dangers of further explosions. They man their boats at the side of the burning battleship to help extinguish the blaze.

7

The U.S. Home Front, 1941 to 1945

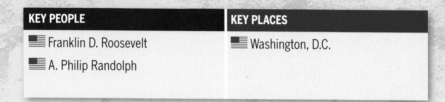

KEY PEOPLE	**KEY PLACES**
🏳 Franklin D. Roosevelt	🏳 Washington, D.C.
🏳 A. Philip Randolph	

The day after the Japanese attacked Pearl Harbor on December 7, 1941, the United States declared war on Japan. On December 11 Germany and Italy declared war on the United States. Having kept itself neutral while at the same time supplying the Allies, the United States was now a full participant in the worldwide conflict. The involvement of the mightiest nation on Earth was to prove decisive. Eventually, U.S. strength and wealth would overwhelm Japan and help overwhelm Germany and its allies. At home, too, American involvement was to have great effects.

War Scares and Japanese Attacks

News of the raid at Pearl Harbor spread rapidly through the United States. Federal Bureau of Investigation director J. Edgar Hoover received a phone call from his Honolulu agent, who held the telephone out the window so that Hoover could hear the explosions. At 1:20 p.m. in Philadelphia, local radio programs were interrupted with news of the Japanese strike. The National Broadcasting Company waited until its 2:30 p.m, eastern time, regular news broadcasts. The Columbia Broadcasting System made its first announcement before the regularly scheduled 3:00 p.m. New York Philharmonic concert broadcast.

Because of the time zone changes, news reached California and the West Coast early in the morning. Widespread panic set in. It seemed to people that a Japanese invasion or air attack might be imminent. In San Francisco, the streets filled with nervous people. As evening fell, they started smashing headlights on street cars and stoning the flashing lights on the marquee of the United Artists Theater to create a blackout. FBI agents rounded up all known Japanese-American males at their homes and sent them to jail, where they remained for several days. Recruiting stations were mobbed by men wanting to get into the active military.

After the attack on Pearl Harbor, the number of personnel in the United States military increased dramatically. By the end of the war, more than 11 million Americans were in military uniform.

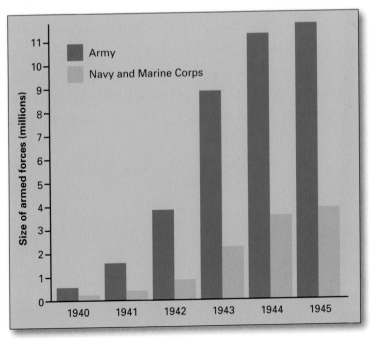

In the capital, the army installed antiaircraft guns on the roofs of government buildings, at Secret Service request. Many antiaircraft guns were replicas, since there was a shortage of actual weapons. Both American coasts were potentially vulnerable. People on the Pacific worried about carrier-based Japanese bombers. On the Atlantic coast the concern was about German submarines. In the course of the war U-boats in the Atlantic and the Gulf of Mexico sank many ships near the U. S. coastline. As far as 6 miles (10 km) out to sea, the vessels were silhouetted against lights on shore from cities such as Miami, Florida. In February 1942 the U.S. Navy destroyer *Jacob Jones* was sunk off Cape May, New Jersey. It was the first American warship sunk in home waters since the Civil War. One U-boat surfaced and sent shells into Atlantic City, New Jersey.

In February 1942 the U.S. Navy destroyer Jacob Jones *was sunk off Cape May, New Jersey.*

In March the office of the Economic Mobilizer, James Byrnes, called for blackouts. They were known as "Byrne-outs" in the affected cities. Homeowners were told to hide their lights at night. As far inland as St. Paul, Minnesota, stores sold special blackout paint for windows. Black sateen was in demand for blackout draperies. Air-raid wardens, wearing white helmets and armed with flashlights, patrolled the streets to enforce blackout regulations.

Early fears about Japanese assaults on the West Coast proved unfounded. In the entire war only four bombs fell from enemy aircraft onto American soil. They were dropped on the forests of Oregon, near the town of Brookings, in September 1942. These raids were flown by Warrant Officer Nobuo Fujita in a small floatplane launched from a submarine a few miles offshore. The purpose of Fujita's bombs was to start forest fires that would divert U.S. resources from the Pacific War. The bombs had little effect.

On the East Coast, the Germans' most daring raid came in June 1942. U-boats attempted to land eight English-speaking spies on Long Island and at Jacksonville, Florida. The spies—including two U.S. citizens—had been trained in Germany to blow up bridges, factories, and transportation routes. They were captured before they reached shore, however. Six were executed and two sentenced to life in prison.

THE OFFICE OF CIVILIAN DEFENSE

In May 1941 Roosevelt issued an Executive Order establishing the Office of Civilian Defense (OCD). The agency was shaped by a report written by his wife, Eleanor, and Florence Kerr, head of Works Progress Administration Community Service Projects. The report proposed that civil defense could promote social reform by encouraging women volunteers to organize community services.

The purpose of the OCD was to protect the American population, to maintain morale, and to recruit civilians for volunteer defense duties. Those duties included setting up air-raid procedures and supervising blackouts. OCD also monitored community needs, such as day care for working mothers and welfare services.

Eleanor Roosevelt's involvement led to charges of political favoritism. Southern politicians rejected her attempt to integrate the agency's programs. She resigned in February 1942. The agency's offices closed in June 1944, and it was abolished the following year.

Organizing the War Economy

The United States was largely safe from enemy attack. It was protected by two oceans that isolated it from Europe and Asia. For many Americans, the greatest impact of the war would come in changes to their work patterns. As in the nations of Europe, the United States mobilized the whole nation for the war effort. The struggle was as much one of economics, labor, and resources as it was of strategy. The government attempts to organize military production proved to be the biggest federal involvement in the economy in the nation's history.

The U.S. entered the war already partly prepared for conflict. Under the leadership of Franklin D. Roosevelt, who had committed the nation to becoming the "arsenal of democracy," U.S. factories and shipyards were geared up for military production under the Lend–Lease agreements of March 1941. Automakers including Chrysler, General Motors, and Ford were making M-3 tanks and B-25 bombers to sell to the Allies.

Industrial factories switched entirely to war production and began seven-day-a-week, twenty-four-hour operations. From 1941 to 1942 the U.S. defense budget grew from $10 billion to $52 billion. By 1943 U.S. shipyards were producing 500 cargo and supply ships every month. In 1942 U.S. factories produced 60,000 aircraft. In 1943 that figure rose to 86,000, and the next year to 96,000.

Defense jobs were everywhere. For example, a St. Paul, Minnesota, mayonnaise manufacturer converted its plant to one that soldered nameplates on gun mounts. Underwood, the typewriter manufacturer, produced M-1 rifles. When a typewriter shortage resulted, civilians were asked to donate personal typewriters to the government. Civilians were also asked to turn over their binoculars to the navy, and their dogs to the army's K-9 Corps.

The government set up a series of agencies to allocate valuable natural resources. Eventually these agencies were consolidated as the War Production Board (WPB). Through the agency's Controlled Materials Plan, aluminum, copper, and steel were divided among various agencies for distribution. Production of nonessential goods, such as new cars, refrigerators, and tennis balls, was halted.

Despite these measures, full defense-related production caused shortages of raw materials. National drives to collect scrap from tin cans to old tires and other rubber products were widespread. Rubber was in such short supply that rubber bands disappeared entirely, replaced by adhesive tape.

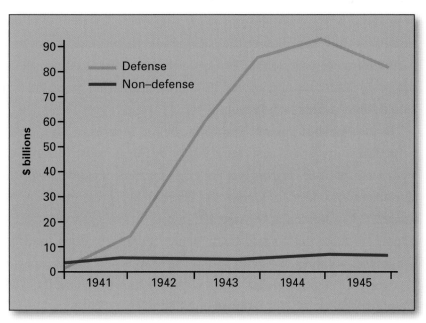

Between 1941 and 1945, spending for defense accelerated significantly. The expenditures peaked in late 1944.

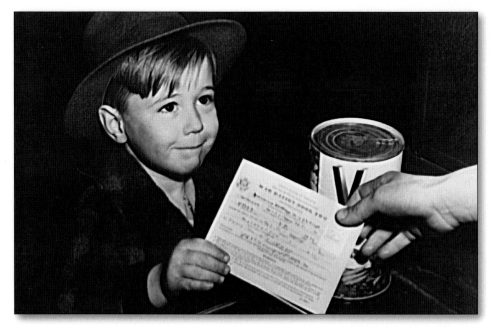

The WPB represented a whole new level of government control of the U.S. economy, even compared with World War I. It bought $16 billion of facilities to convert to war production. The WPB controlled prices, pay rates, transportation routes, and set quotas for production in industry and food.

Agriculture, which had been one of the poorest sectors in the U.S. economy in the 1930s, profited from increased demand. Rather than reduce surpluses, as they had during the Depression, farmers now sought to make their land more productive. The government subsidized production. Then the government bought nearly half of all the butter, meat, fruit, and vegetables that farmers produced.

Improved equipment, planning, better fertilizers and pest controls helped farmers to increase their yields by 30 percent. To replace laborers who were mobilized into the services, farmers imported labor from the Caribbean and Mexico. Under the Bracero Agreement of July 1942, more than 200,000 Mexicans became temporary workers in the United States. These workers harvested fruit, sugar beets, tomatoes, and lettuce in California; potatoes in Idaho; and apples and wheat in Washington.

The war economy did away with the last traces of the Depression. Unemployment, at 17.2 percent in 1939, fell by 1944 to a low of 1.2 percent. Likewise, in 1939 Americans earned a total of $72.8 billion; by 1944 that figure had soared to $165.3 billion. Such increases were generally not matched by a rise in the standard of living, since there were few consumer goods for people to buy. As a result, American workers saved a total of $150 billion from 1941 to 1945.

Rationing and Consumption

The increase in U.S. war productivity was the basis of Allied victory in World War II. On the home front, however, it forced Americans to give up many conveniences. Rationing became a feature of daily life for the first time. From 1942 on, ten essential goods were rationed. Within a year 5,600 rationing boards limited a wide range of products. Families received ration tickets and books according to a points system; the tickets allowed each family a weekly total of 4 ounces (113 g) of butter, 4 pounds (1.6 kg) of cheese, and 28 ounces (800 g) of meat.

Other rationed foodstuffs included sugar, coffee, flour, fish, and canned goods. It was impossible to get hold of imported goods such as spices, tea, and wine. Tuesday and Friday were declared meatless days. Eggs and vegetables became popular replacements for red meat. The general nutrition levels of the country actually improved as Americans ate less fat and meat and more vegetables and carbohydrates. A popular way to

The Office of War Information distributed posters such as this one from May 1942. The poster calls for patriotic rationing during the wartime emergency.

supplement rations was to plant a "victory garden" to grow produce on any spare patch of ground. An estimated 40 percent of the vegetables eaten in wartime America were grown in such gardens.

Food was not the only item affected by government-imposed shortages. New cars were forbidden, and restrictions on gasoline, tires, and spare parts were tight. Paper shortages meant that the army introduced a system named V-mail. Letters were photographed and sent at a reduced size. Most people stopped sending Christmas cards to save cardboard. A popular slogan urged consumers "Use it up, wear it out, make it do, or do without."

> *"Use it up, wear it out, make it do, or do without."*

Another item rationed was cloth. The government regulated the length of fabric, and forbade fashion details that used extra cloth, such as pleats, extra pockets, deep hems, or hoods. Zippers were also forbidden. Makeup and hair products were in short supply, as were silk stockings, even after the invention of the artificial fabric nylon. Women sometimes used eyeliner to draw a "seam" on the back of their leg to imitate silk stockings. Most Americans bore such sacrifices willingly. Their deprivation was minor compared with that suffered by people in Allied Europe. Rationing was also a reminder to many people of the hard times of the Great Depression. Their efforts bound people together and made a clear contribution to the war effort. Some people, however, ignored the restrictions. A vast black market thrived throughout the war, despite government campaigns to the contrary.

The War and U.S. Labor

The demand for labor led to many changes in the U.S. economy. With so many Anglo-American males called into the military, women and ethnic minorities became an important source of labor. Factory workers' wages rose by 15 percent in 1942, although the average work week was lengthened to forty-eight hours to increase production. Unions largely agreed with management during the war. Employers were eager to keep their workers so they offered perks such as music in the workplace.

Many workers moved during the war, mostly to take up manufacturing jobs in the north or in California, the home of many defense facilities.

Small towns grew overnight, and the suburbs of northern cities were overwhelmed by the arrival of new workers. The population influx placed strains on local schools, hospitals, housing, and other facilities. In many places, local inhabitants resented the newcomers.

The situation was worsened when intensified by racial tension. Hundreds of thousands of black Americans moved from the South to northern cities during the war to seek work. In the North they found poor, cramped living conditions with high rents. They had to pay high prices for goods that were in short supply. Traditional black neighborhoods began to spill out into the surrounding areas, often causing resentment among white residents. These feelings sometimes led to violence.

Women and the War Effort

At the start of the war, the popular image of a woman's role in America was as a housewife, keeping the family and household together while American men were away fighting. Women voluntarily collected metal and other household waste for recycling. They worked for the Red Cross and kept household consumption as low as possible. By 1942, however, it was clear that industry needed more workers. All males who were not in the armed services were already at work. The War Manpower Commission (WMC), created in 1942, helped bring 7 million women into the workforce. They joined the 12 million women already working.

These two women are World War II examples of "Rosie the Riveter." At work assembling planes for the Douglas Aircraft Company of Long Beach, California, they represent two of fifty-eight different nationalities that contributed to the war effort.

At first, the WMC was worried that women would not want to leave their traditional roles. Advertising campaigns promised that working women would hasten the war's end and bring their husbands home and life could return to normal.

One of the most famous government campaigns starred "Rosie the Riveter." Appearing on posters with her sleeves rolled up and her hair tucked underneath a scarf, Rosie encouraged women to work in war production industries with her slogan, "We Can Do It!" Women took many jobs in industry, from welding and riveting to assembling bombers and tanks. Women did not take part in combat, but they served in the armed services as part of the Women's Army Corps (WACs).

The War and Civil Rights

African-American troops of the 92nd Infantry division threw back a 1944 German attack in the hills around Viareggio, Italy. Here, Lieutenant General Lucian Truscott, commanding general of the Fifth Army in Italy, commends them for their bravery.

When the war began, there were about 13 million African Americans in the U.S. They made up about 10 percent of the U.S. population. Although they were still treated as second-class citizens, black Americans had begun to press for voting rights and other changes. Black leaders saw economic strength as the key to winning civil rights for African Americans. Over the course of the war the largest black organization, the National Association for the Advancement of Colored People (NAACP), increased its membership ninefold to more than 450,000.

Many African Americans at first viewed the war effort with suspicion, if not outright cynicism. African-American efforts on the home front during World War I had brought little in the way of better civil rights. Often without the vote, African Americans still did not always enjoy the full benefits of the democracy America was fighting for in Europe.

In Franklin D. Roosevelt and, in particular, Eleanor Roosevelt, black Americans had strong allies. President Roosevelt's famous "black cabinet" brought to Washington more than one hundred outstanding African-

American advisers, such as Mary McCleod Bethune, to influence government policy. Eleanor Roosevelt made high-profile demonstrations of her belief in equal rights.

She invited the famous black opera singer Marian Anderson to perform at the White House after Anderson had been forbidden to sing at Constitution Hall in Washington, D.C. by the Daughters of the American Revolution. However, progress in civil rights was still slow. President Roosevelt refused to introduce an antilynching law that he thought would cause him to lose support of southern Democrats. In the early years of the New Deal, too, its agencies often seemed to discriminate in allocating housing, employment, or welfare.

POLITICAL WORLD — THE GI BILL OF RIGHTS

On July 28, 1943, Franklin D. Roosevelt used one of his regular radio broadcasts to announce that the government was planning how to bring service personnel back into civilian life after the war: "They must not be demobilized into an environment of inflation and unemployment, to a place on the bread line or on a corner selling apples."

His announcement reflected a determination to avoid the problems that had followed demobilization after World War I (1914 to 1918). Throughout the 1920s and 1930s veterans of the conflict, led by the American Legion, asked for better compensation for their service. In 1932, 20,000 veterans marched on the capital to press their claims. These "bonus marchers" were met with troops and tanks. After he became president, Roosevelt himself refused to increase pensions to veterans.

However, Roosevelt was worried about what would happen after soldiers returned home from the current war. Government committees convinced him that veterans deserved special treatment. In April 1944 Congress passed what became known as the "GI Bill of Rights." The bill provided veterans with many benefits. These included guidance in finding a career, preference in hiring for some jobs, and cash allowances while they looked for work; full tuition fees and expenses for education; and loans for buying homes or starting businesses. Later, the bill was expanded to provide medical care and more veterans' hospitals. The program was run by the new Veterans' Administration.

Within a decade of the war's end, more than half of all who had left the armed services had benefited from the bill. The bill smoothed the return of soldiers to civilian life, and avoided the mass unemployment and economic hardship that Roosevelt's planners had feared.

The NAACP led demands that the armed forces at last be integrated. At the start of the war African-American recruits could only join one of the Army's four blacks-only units, created in 1866. Roosevelt eventually increased the number of black service personnel, but still refused to integrate the armed services. He accepted army insistence that such a move would negatively affect morale and discipline. Black troops ate and traveled separately from whites. In some military camps they complained that they were less free than German prisoners of war.

Most black service personnel filled support roles, as railroad or dockyard workers. The army's leaders were reluctant to put black troops in conflict. Those blacks who did see active service, however, did well. The 332nd Fighter Group, known as the Lonely Eagles, won the Presidential Unit Citation in March 1945. Its 405 elite black pilots shot down 409 enemy aircraft. A turning point came toward the end of the war, after the invasion of France on June 6, 1944. By then, the armed forces were so short of white tank crews that they called for black volunteers. More than 500 were led into battle by the distinguished African-American officer Lieutenant General Benjamin O. Davis, Sr.

Most black service personnel filled support roles. . .

On the home front, meanwhile, early "help wanted" ads for the defense industries specified that applicants be "Nordic" or from "north European stock." Such discrimination largely affected the many black Americans who had moved from the South to northern cities in search of work. In 1940 unemployment among blacks stood at 25 percent.

In 1941 A. Philip Randolph proposed a march on Washington, D. C., to protest employment discrimination and to insist that the defense industry be opened to black Americans. Backed by the NAACP, he wanted to bring hundreds of thousands of blacks from around the country to the federal capital. Roosevelt sought to avoid a demonstration at a time when he was asking the nation to pull together. When he called Randolph to the White House demanding that he call off the protest, Randolph replied, "The plants must be opened to negroes, Mr. President, or I must let my people march."

In response Roosevelt created the Fair Employment Practices Commission (FEPC). Randolph called off the march. The FEPC was intended to protect black Americans from discrimination in hiring. By 1944, 2 million African Americans worked in the defense industry. However, those lucky enough to find work still did not escape discrimination. They earned less than their white counterparts, and suffered from poor housing and living conditions. In some areas African Americans took to the streets in violent protest. In June 1943 a series of fistfights between whites and blacks in Detroit, where the Ku Klux Klan had been causing trouble, escalated into widespread violence. African-American homes and cars were destroyed. White mobs attacked blacks getting off work and beat and stripped them. Groups from both sides roamed the streets, looting stores, taking guns and ammunition from pawnshops, and tipping over cars. After twenty-four hours Detroit police reported twenty-three dead—eight of them African Americans shot by the police—over 700 injured, and 600 in jail. It took 6,000 army troops to restore order.

Groups from both sides roamed the streets, looting stores, taking guns and ammunition from pawnshops, and tipping over cars.

One positive aspect of the civil rights battle was an attempt to eliminate the poll tax, levied by southern states in exchange for the right to vote. If a person's grandparents had been voters, the tax was waived. This meant whites who had voting ancestors in the Civil War could vote tax-free, but African Americans, who were legally entitled to vote but sometimes could not afford the tax, found it difficult. In 1943 a New York representative introduced a bill to eliminate the tax. Southerners, however, fought it and managed to defeat the bill for the time being.

Treatment of "Enemy Aliens"

African-American rights were severely limited before and during the conflict. There was also mistreatment of other ethnic groups, particularly Japanese Americans. Although there were no known cases of Japanese Americans being involved in spying or sabotage, white suspicion of the Japanese made it easy for army leaders to portray them as potential subversives. Concerned with other affairs, Roosevelt allowed General John L. De Witt, army commander on the West Coast in February 1942, to round up some

110,000 Japanese Americans in California, western Oregon, western Washington, and the southern half of Arizona.

De Witt forced the Japanese Americans into ten detention camps made up of mass barracks and mess halls surrounded by barbed wire and gun towers. Internal government memos referred to the camps as "concentration camps," but the army publically called them "war-duration relocation centers." Two of the camps were in Arkansas, while the rest were in desert lands or on Indian reservations in western states. Voluntary migration east was allowed. But most Japanese Americans were limited to taking out $100 a month from their bank accounts. Since no government aid was offered, few could afford to move.

Most Japanese Americans who had built up businesses lost everything they owned.

On March 26, 1942, De Witt revoked all Japanese-American travel permits. He ordered those who had moved to wait to be relocated by the army. Most Japanese Americans who had built up businesses lost everything they owned. They were forced to sell their homes for rock-bottom prices and could bring very little with them. Young Japanese men could volunteer for military service, and a Japanese-American unit that served in Italy brought home a large number of honors. However, the rest were not allowed to leave the camps until December 1944. Most who returned to their old property found it gone. Others faced danger from white mobs, who beat them and set fire to their new homes. No Italian Americans or German Americans, who were also officially termed "enemy aliens," were so singled out.

Racial prejudice was also found in Southern California. Teenagers there, mostly Mexicans, liked to wear "zoot suits" made up of a long jacket and trousers tightly pegged at the cuff, with deep pleats at the waist and wide knees. In mid-1943 local soldiers and sailors from the Chavez Ravine naval base went into the Mexican districts, beating up anybody found in such a suit and stripping them. Civilian and military police looked the other way, or sometimes actually jailed the victims. These riots went on for days until they were brought under control.

The OWI and National Morale

One of the U.S. government's concerns at the start of the conflict was how to maintain national morale. In June 1942 Roosevelt created the Office of War Information (OWI). Under its director, Elmer Davis, the OWI's domestic branch educated Americans about the ideological conflict behind the war. The overseas branch directed its messages toward a foreign audience.

The OWI's portrayal of the war stressed the evils of Fascism and the importance of its defeat. Roosevelt was portrayed as a great leader of a free people, with many achievements in his 1930s New Deal. To Roosevelt's

POLITICAL WORLD: THE 1944 ELECTION

The presidential election of 1944 was the first since the U. S. entered the war. The election gave Americans their chance to judge Franklin D. Roosevelt's leadership. The midterm congressional election of 1942 had resulted in Republican gains in both the House and Senate. Roosevelt minimized any damage to himself by remaining largely aloof from party politics. Now, however, he sought a fourth term of office.

The Republican candidate in 1944 was Thomas E. Dewey (1902–1971). In the late 1930s Dewey rose to fame as New York's special prosecutor, taking on gangsters such as Lucky Luciano and Dutch Schultz. As governor of New York, Dewey was a leading critic of Roosevelt. However, he had also gained a reputation as a new kind of Republican, a social liberal who supported civil rights and welfare laws.

Dewey and Roosevelt disliked one another—the president referred to his opponent as "the little man." Dewey, meanwhile, refused to believe that Roosevelt had not known in advance about the attack on Pearl Harbor. George C. Marshall, chief of staff of the U.S. Army, asked Dewey to leave the issue out of the campaign. Dewey agreed but argued that "Instead of being reelected, [Roosevelt] ought to be impeached." The two parties also agreed that there would be no discussion of any disagreement over Roosevelt's idea to create a new international organization—the United Nations—after the war.

Instead, Dewey attacked "the mess in Washington," the president's "tired old men," and the New Deal, which he said had done little to lessen unemployment in the 1930s. Dewey's attacks damaged Roosevelt, who was forced to engage in the political debate to rebut them. Although an upset looked possible, on election day, November 7, Roosevelt won with 53.5 percent of the vote, his narrowest margin of victory in a presidential election. Although he was not as popular with Americans as before, they still believed that he could and should lead them to victory.

critics, particularly in Congress, the OWI seemed as if it were a political body trying to influence American voters to appreciate FDR more.

One of the OWI's most visible areas of operation was in the movie industry. The Bureau of Motion Pictures wanted Hollywood to portray the United States as a harmonious place. In the three years of its existence, the OWI changed parts of more than 500 movies to bring the films in line with official policy.

Broadway musicals were also popular. *Oklahoma!*, which opened in 1943, was sold out for years. The theater maintained a policy that military personnel in uniform could get free standing-room tickets. The war even affected newspaper comic strips. Most of the heroes of strips such as *Terry and the Pirates* and *Joe Palooka* went into uniform. Shortages were a continuing problem in the story lines of the strip *Gasoline Alley*.

President Roosevelt insisted that professional sports continue throughout the war. But play suffered as many of the best athletes served in the

A poster advertising U.S. war bonds as a way to aid the war effort. War bonds offered Americans a financial and moral stake in the war.

armed forces. Baseball lost such major attractions as Ted Williams, Joe DiMaggio, Hank Greenberg, and Bob Feller to wartime service. Many of these players never got a chance to set the records they might have, had their careers not been interrupted.

Football teams were so reduced that in Pennsylvania, Pittsburgh's Steelers and Philadelphia's Eagles merged for a season to form the Steeagles. Professional golf gained in popularity, but because of travel restrictions and the top golfers' service in the military, no Professional Golfer's Association (PGA) tournaments were held in 1942 or 1943. Many horse racetracks closed because gasoline rationing made attendance difficult. Elsewhere, wagering in 1943 and 1944 rose to record levels.

Baseball lost such major attractions as Ted Williams, Joe DiMaggio, Hank Greenberg, and Bob Feller to wartime service.

Thirty million homes had radios, and broadcast news was a major business. Both newspapers and radio news became so important that journalism began to be treated more seriously. Journalism schools raised their standards and journalists' salaries increased.

Many of the big bands that had been popular in the prewar years broke up. Bandleader Glenn Miller went into the army and was lost in a plane crash in the English Channel toward the end of the war. Singers became more the rage, especially a young Frank Sinatra, whose punctured eardrum kept him out of the military. Unpopular with the older generation, he appealed to so many teenagers that he made over $1 million a year from his records, personal appearances, and radio shows.

The war had an effect on every part of American life, including religion. Churches generally threw themselves into the war effort. Some 8,000 ordained individuals became chaplains in the armed services. Churches at home raised money, distributed Bibles, aided soldiers away from home, and provided volunteers to war service agencies. Despite this, however, organized religion as an institution continued to decline in importance in forming public opinion and providing leadership to the public.

Timeline

1929 • Heinrich Himmler takes control of the SS (*Shutzstaffel*).

1933 • Hitler comes to power in Germany.

1934 • The SS controls concentration camps.
  • Hitler becomes leader of Nazi Party following "Night of the Long Knives."

1936 • The SS gains control of Germany's police force and intelligence services.

1939 • Germany invades Poland.
  • Plot to assassinate Hitler fails.
  • Italy and Germany sign Pact of Steel.
  • Britain initiates the draft.
  • Denmark signs nonaggression treaty with Germany.
  • Spain signs Anti-Comintern Pact.

1940 • France falls to Germany.
  • Italy invades Greece and fails.
  • Britain passes Emergency Powers Act.
  • Germany's Blitz of Britain begins.
  • Germany invades Denmark.

1941 • Germany invades Russia.
  • Tojo becomes Japan's prime minister.
  • Stalin delivers "scorch the earth" radio broadcast.
  • Germany begins siege of Leningrad.
  • Britain drafts young women.
  • British use the first escort carrier to
  • protect convoys in shipping routes.
  • British break German U-boat codes.
  • Japan attacks Pearl Harbor.
  • U.S. declares war on Japan and Germany.
  • President Roosevelt creates the Fair Employment Practices Commission.

1942 • Germany launches Operation Drumroll.
  • Wannsee Conference determines the "Final Solution," the extermination of the Jews.
  • Allies bomb German cities—Lübeck, Rostok, Cologne.
  • Germans retaliate with "Baedecker" raids against historic British towns.
  • RAF bombers use TR 1335, the "Gee," as electronic aid.
  • U.S. Japanese sent to internment camps.
  • President Roosevelt creates the Office of War Information.
  • Mexico declares war on Germany, Italy, and Japan.

1943 • War begins to turn against Axis powers.
  • RAF begins night bombing of German targets.
  • Italy loses African empire.
  • Allies launch Operation Husky, the Invasion of Sicily.
  • Allies launch invasion of Italy.
  • Mussolini deposed from Italian leadership, arrested, and imprisoned.
  • Hitler rescues Mussolini in Operation Oak.
  • Italy surrenders to Allies; Allied invasion against occupying German forces continues in Operations Baytown, Avalanche, and Slapstick.
  • Allies stalemated in drive to the Gustav Line in Italy.
  • Allies defeat German U-boat attacks in Battle of the Atlantic.
  • Allies sink Germany's *Scharnhorst*.

1944 • President Roosevelt elected to historic fourth term.

Bibliography

Alford, Kenneth, and Theodore P. Savas. *Nazi Millionaires: The Allied Search for Hidden SS Gold.* Havertown, Pennsylvania: Casemate Publishers, 2002.

Arnold, Simone. *Facing the Lion: Memoirs of a Young Girl in Nazi Europe.* New Orleans, Louisiana: Grammaton Press, 2000.

Bowman, Martin W. *B-17 Flying Fortresses of the Eighth Air Force.* Oxford, UK: Osprey Publishing Ltd, 2002.

Coyne, Kevin. *Marching Home: To War and Back with the Men of One American Town.* New York: Penguin, 2003.

Evans, Mark L. *Great World War II Battles in the Arctic.* Westport, Connecticut: Greenwood Publishing Group, 1999.

Ford, Roger. *The Sherman Tank.* St. Paul, Minnesota: Motorbooks International, 1999.

Frank, Anne. *The Diary of a Young Girl.* New York: Prentice Hall, 1993.

Hogg, Ian. *Great Land Battles of World War II.* London: Blandford Press, 1987.

Inada, Lawson Fusao. *Only What We Could Carry: The Japanese American Internment Experience.* Berkeley, California: Heyday Books, 2000.

Johnson, Eric A. *Nazi Terror: The Gestapo, Jews, and Ordinary Germans.* New York: Basic Books, 2000.

Kaplan, Marion A. *Between Dignity and Despair: Jewish Life in Nazi Germany* (Studies in Jewish History). NY: Oxford University Press, 1998.

MacLachlan, Ian. *USAAF Fighter Stories: Dramatic Accounts of American Fighter Pilots in Training and Combat over Europe in World War II.* Yeovil, UK: Haynes Publishing, 1997.

Mann, Chris, and Christer Jorgensen. *Arctic War.* New York: St. Martin's Press, 2003.

Middlebrook, Martin. *The Peenemünde Road.* London: Cassell Academic, 2001.

Montagu, Ewen. *The Man Who Never Was: World War II's Boldest Counter Intelligence Operation.* Annapolis, Maryland: The United States Naval Institute Press, 2001.

Murray, Williamson. *Luftwaffe, 1933–45.* Dulles, Virginia: Brasseys, 1996.

Mussolini, Benito, et al. *My Rise and Fall.* New York: Da Capo Press, September 1998.

Patton, George S. *War As I Knew It.* New York: Mariner Books (Houghton Mifflin), 1995.

Potter, Elmer Belmont. *Nimitz.* Annapolis, Maryland: The Unites States Naval Institute Press, 1988.

Rommel, Erwin, et al. *The Rommel Papers.* New York: Da Capo Press, 1988.

Smith, Denis Mack. *Mussolini.* New York: Sterling Publications, 2002.

Speer, Albert, et al. *Inside the Third Reich: Memoirs.* New York: Touchstone Books, 1997.

Stein, George H. *The Waffen SS: Hitler's Elite Guard at War, 1939–1945.* Ithaca, New York: Cornell University Press, 2001.

Voss, Johan. *Black Edelweiss: A Memoir of Combat and Conscience by a Soldier of the Waffen-SS.* Bedford, Pennsylvania: The Aberjona Press, 2002.

Werner, Herbert A. *Iron Coffins: A Personal Account of the German U-Boat Battles of World War II.* New York: Henry Holt, 1969.

Further Information

BOOKS

Heinrichs, Ann. *The Internment of Japanese Americans: Innocence, Guilt, and Wartime Justice* (Perspectives On). New York: Marshall Cavendish, 2010.

Holm, Tim. *Code Talkers and Warriors: Native Americans and World War II* (Landmark Events in Native American History). New York: Chelsea House, 2007.

Jensen, Richard, and Tim McNeese, eds. *World War II 1939-1945* (Discovering U.S. History). New York: Chelsea House, 2010.

Williams, Barbara. *World War II: Pacific* (Chronicle of America's Wars). Minneapolis: Lerner Publications, 2004.

WEBSITES

www.wwiimemorial.com
The U.S. National World War II Memorial.

www.hitler.org
The Hitler Historical Museum is a nonpolitical, educational resource for the study of Hitler and Nazism.

http://gi.grolier.com/wwii/wwii_ mainpage.html
The story of World War II, with biographies, articles, photographs, and films.

www.ibiblio.org/pha
Original documents on all aspects of the war.

DVDS

Great Fighting Machines of World War II. Arts Magic, 2007.

The War: A Film by Ken Burns and Lynn Novick. PBS Home Video, 2007.

World War II 360°. A & E Television Networks, 2009.

Index

NOTE: Page numbers in **bold** refer to photographs or illustrations.